Views from on High

Views from on High

Fire Tower Trails
in the Adirondacks and Catskills

by JOHN P. FREEMAN
with Wesley H. Haynes

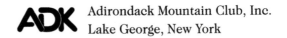 Adirondack Mountain Club, Inc.
Lake George, New York

Design by Susanne Murtha, Apropos Design Solutions
Cover photo © 2001 by Carl Heilman II
Text photos by the author unless noted otherwise
Typography by Michele Phillips
Page maps by Karen Brooks and Therese S. Brosseau, updates by Linda DeMasi

This book was made possible with the generous support of the Lillian M. Slater
Charitable Trust. The Glens Falls–Saratoga Chapter of the Adirondack Mountain Club provided significant additional funding.

Published by the Adirondack Mountain Club
814 Goggins Road, Lake George, New York 12845-4117
www.adk.org

The Adirondack Mountain Club (ADK) is dedicated to the protection and
responsible recreational use of the New York State Forest Preserve, parks, and
other wild lands and waters. The Club, founded in 1922, is a member-directed
organization committed to public service and stewardship. ADK employs a
balanced approach to outdoor recreation, advocacy, environmental education,
and natural resource conservation.

Library of Congress Cataloguing-in-Publication Data
Freeman, John P., 1937–
    Views from on high : fire tower trails in the Adirondacks and Catskills/
John P. Freeman with Wesley H. Haynes.
    p. cm.
Includes index.
ISBN 0-935272-96-8 (pbk.)
    1.Hiking—New York (State)—Adirondack Park—Guidebooks. 2. Hiking—
New York (State)—Catskill Forest Preserve—Guidebooks. 3. Fire lookout
stations—New York (State)—Adirondack Park—History. 4. Fire lookout
stations—New York (State)—Catskill Forest Preserve—History.
5. Adirondack Park (N.Y.)—Guidebooks. 6. Catskill Forest Preserve (N.Y.)—
Guidebooks. I. Haynes, Wesley. II. Title.

GV199.42.N652 A3429 2001
796.51'09747—dc21

2001035540

Printed in Canada
10 09   4 5 6 7 8 9 10

Dedication

This guidebook is dedicated to the countless forest fire observers who staffed the more than sixty observation sites in these rugged mountains from about 1910 until 1990. They watched from their lonely perches and answered myriad questions from curious hikers about the view, the forest, the wildlife, and much more. They served well the people of New York State.

Contents

We Welcome Your Letters!

ADK and its authors make every effort to keep our guidebook information current, however, trail conditions are always changing. If you note an error or discrepancy, or you wish to forward a suggestion, we welcome your input. Please write the Adirondack Mountain Club, Attn: Publications, or e-mail us at <pubs@adk.org>. Cite the book title, year of your edition and printing (see copyright page), page number, and date of your observations. Thanks for your help!

Fire Tower Summits
within the Adirondack Park

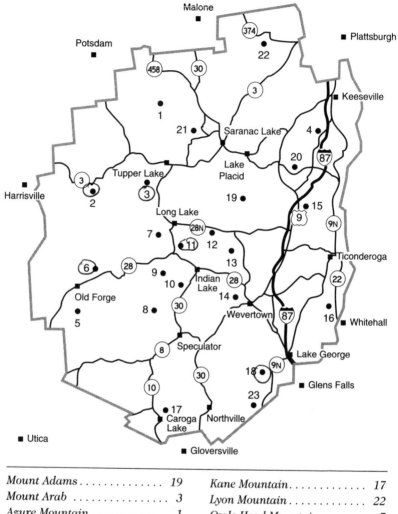

Fire Tower Summits within the Catskill Park

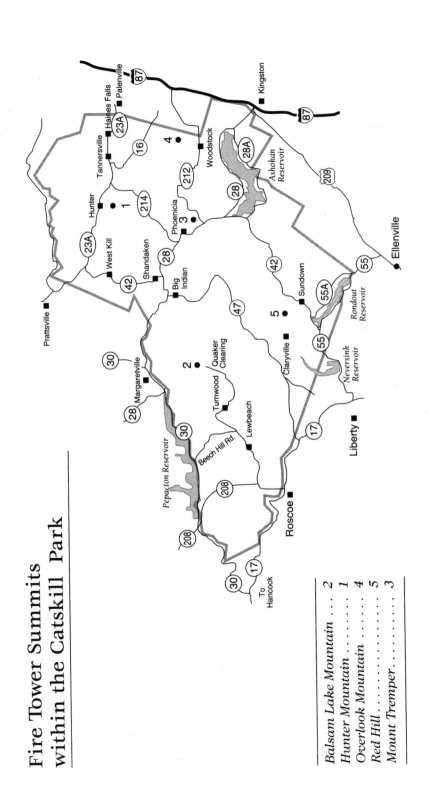

Balsam Lake Mountain 2
Hunter Mountain 1
Overlook Mountain 4
Red Hill 5
Mount Tremper 3

Balsam Lake Mountain tower. In the course of the tower's restoration, members of the local ironworkers union volunteered to replace cross braces. John Stanger of Wind Energy Power Company of Cragsmoor also donated time and expertise toward ironwork installation.

Preface

FIRE TOWERS! The view from these wonderful mountaintop locations is always marvelous. We pick out the summits of familiar peaks around the horizon. We ask the fire observer stationed in the tower's cab for the names of those we don't recognize. He or she (some were women) shows us the alidade, a small mounted telescope used to get an exact directional sighting on smoke. We marvel at the vast expanse of forested terrain. We reflect on the wisdom of our forebears who saw the need to preserve the "north woods" for water conservation and recreation.

Today, this scene is largely gone. Oh, not the forest and the mountains; they are still there. But the fire tower *observers* are indeed gone. The last of the observers left their stations after the summer of 1990. Of the approximately sixty-nine towers that were once on the peaks of the Catskill and Adirondack Parks, only twenty-three remain in the Adirondacks and five in the Catskills. Several of the Adirondack towers are on borrowed time.

Why have the observers disappeared? First, the New York State Department of Environmental Conservation (DEC), responsible for operation of the Forest Preserve and for park fire suppression, determined from its records that ninety percent of fires were being reported not from fire towers but from ground observers, many of them private citizens. There is also less of a threat from fire these days compared to the early 1900s, when railroad engines sparked many fires and clear-cut slash provided the means for the flames to spread. The maturing forest is able to retain moisture and thereby lessen the risk of wildfire. In drought conditions, the state can commission private pilots to check the woods.

When the observers left, the towers were abandoned by the DEC. With no one to maintain them, they decayed rapidly, like old houses, and some were eventually dismantled. The public's renewed sense of the value of wilderness, as reflected in the State Land Master Plans for the two Forest Preserve parks, has led to removal of other fire towers on lands classified as Wilderness in 1971.

In the Adirondack Park

This guidebook describes the Adirondack fire tower summits in two distinct categories. The first eighteen towers are all situated on land in the New York State Forest Preserve zoned as Wild Forest or on land within the Adirondack Park belonging to not-for-profit organizations that value the towers' existence and intend to keep them

Blue Line Matters

The "blue line" that defines the Adirondack and Catskill Parks is said to have originated in 1891 when politicians and others proposing the creation of the Adirondack Park outlined its boundaries in blue ink on a New York State map. The term was later extended to the Catskill Park. Today these parks are a patchwork of public and private lands that brings at least as much confusion as joy to residents and visitors alike.

The Forest Preserve comprises the public or state-owned lands, a little less than half the total land area of these parks. This distinction matters to the average hiker because the extensive trails in both parks rely on a combination of public lands and rights-of-way granted by private landowners. In addition, myriad official designations—Wilderness, Wild Forest, Primitive Area, etc.—have their own attendant regulations.

Most of the fire towers described in this book are located on public lands. Where parts of the trails or the trailhead itself is on private land, the owners have given permission for traverse by the hiking public. On these trails and elsewhere in these unique parks, we must respect private landowners' rights and abide by the conditions of use in order to retain the privilege of access.

This curious mixture of public and private lands is an interesting study in tolerance between those people who live and work within the parks and those who live elsewhere but cherish them for their recreational value. Often these groups have come into conflict, but that's another story.

—J.P.F.

open to the public. The Adirondack Park State Land Master Plan (APSLMP), which outlines those uses to which the Forest Preserve may be put, states that fire towers in Wild Forest areas that are no longer being used as active fire lookouts may be retained as long as they serve an educational purpose.

The last five Adirondack summits have towers that are either on private land or on land in the Forest Preserve's Wilderness, Primitive, or Canoe areas where the APSLMP defines them as "nonconforming structures."

The Department of Environmental Conservation can decide at any time to remove the two nonconforming towers, and will likely do so eventually. Towers on private lands may at any time become inaccessible to the public. The dilapidated tower on Mount Adams, now on land owned by IP Industries, may one day become part of the High Peaks Wilderness and thus be slated for removal as a nonconforming structure.

In the Catskill Park

The Catskill Park has but five metal Aermotor towers (see p. 31) remaining, all situated on Wild Forest summits that have almost no views except for those from the towers. These five towers are well-distributed throughout the Park with Overlook to the east, Balsam Lake near the western border, Red Hill on the southern border, Hunter in the north-central, and Mount Tremper about in the middle.

Endangered Towers

The following fire towers are on summits to which hikers have access... for now (spring 2001):

MOUNT ADAMS—On private land, which if it ever comes into the Forest Preserve, will likely be added to the adjoining High Peaks Wilderness Area

HURRICANE MOUNTAIN—"Nonconforming" tower in the Hurricane Mountain Primitive Area

LYON MOUNTAIN—On private timber company lands

SPRUCE MOUNTAIN—Access over private timber company lands; summit owned by Saratoga County

ST. REGIS MOUNTAIN—"Nonconforming" tower in the St. Regis Canoe Area that is slated for removal

Restorations

The year 1993 marks a pivotal year for public realization that a slice of Forest Preserve history was about to slide away. The Adirondack Ecological Center in Newcomb restored a tower on Goodnow Mountain and, in the far southwest corner of the Adirondack Park, citizens rallied to restore the tower on Kane Mountain. In January of that year, the Adirondack Mountain Club (ADK) invited several interested parties to a meeting in the town hall at Indian Lake to discuss how the Blue Mountain fire tower could be restored to safe public use, both as a recreational destination and as an educational site.

Neil Woodworth, ADK's conservation director, advanced this idea for Blue Mountain because it already had about 15,000 yearly visitors from a trailhead on a major paved highway, and its successful rehabilitation could serve as a model for others. A series of meetings ensued, with representatives of the DEC, town of Indian Lake, Adirondack Museum, Adirondack Architectural Heritage (AARCH), and Cornell Cooperative Extension of Hamilton County, among others, actively engaged in the process. By 1995, the Blue Mountain tower had been restored to safe public use and a new group at Hadley set about to restore this Saratoga County town's fire tower, followed by similar efforts in 1996 at Poke-O-Moonshine Mountain and in 1997 at Mount Arab.

Wind of all these efforts blew into the Catskills in 1997 and the Catskill Center for Conservation and Development (CCCD), along with DEC, established a goal to restore all five remaining Catskill towers by the year 2000. Their three-year concerted effort paid off. They reached their goal with fundraising and physical work by five separate volunteer groups using the CCCD as the central repository of contributions.

Back in the Adirondacks, although ten towers are being actively sponsored by local groups in 2003, there is need for additional "Friends" groups to take up the cause of towers on Pillsbury and Wakely Mountains. Without such local interest, it seems inevitable that these particularly interesting towers will deteriorate to the point of no return. See Appendix A, pages 144–146, for each adopted tower's contact.

Educational Value

The various observers, both *in* the towers and *of* the towers, agree that these structures can serve the public by providing opportunities for educational experiences. Education is what the state had in mind when it spent millions on the Visitor Interpretive Centers at Paul Smiths and Newcomb in the Adirondacks. Over the last seven years, eleven towers have been restored at almost no public expense. These natural classrooms provide a unique opportunity for an encounter with an interpreter, or Summit Guide, during the summer hiking season. To date, only the Blue, Hadley, Arab, and Poke-O-Moonshine committees have funded paid interpreters, although many others use volunteers on summer and fall weekends. Blue had a guide for one season and Hadley for five seasons as of summer 2000, funded largely through grants from the International Paper company.

Hikers, many of them children, come to these summits anticipating a tower view. And while they climb, various questions arise among family members, Scout groups, and school groups. Are there bears around here? Can we see Mount Marcy? What kind of rock is the mountain made of? Why are the trees up here so scrawny?

They are told that the endless forests are a mixture of "forever wild" state Forest Preserve lands and private timber lands. But they can't see any boundary lines. In fact, except for the tower, human works are scarcely visible at all.

Tower committees at Goodnow, Blue, Hadley, and Poke-O-Moonshine Mountains have designed nature brochures that hikers can pick up at the trail register. This approach to interpretation and education converts the trail up the mountain to a nature trail with numbered stops along the way. The object of the hike then becomes more than exercise. It becomes a treat for both mind and body.

The State's Role

It is time for our state's political leadership to find money to help more Catskill and Adirondack communities fund educational projects tied to the towers. A two-month summer interpreter (the weekend of July 4 through Labor Day) is about a $2,500 expense. Quick arithmetic demonstrates that less than $38,000 annually would enable all fifteen current tower committees to fund and train a summer interpreter. Assuming that in these two months, each of the fifteen summits sees on average 10,000 hikers, not an unreasonable guess based on DEC's trail register statistics, that's potential contact with 150,000 people eager to know more about this precious natural resource. That's a cost of 25¢ per encounter! Cheap tuition.

A Canonical List for Recreationalists

That leaves for your consideration a list of eighteen Adirondack summits and five Catskill summits that I consider worthy of a canonical list of Forest Preserve fire tower mountains. The most compelling feature of these twenty-three ascents is that the hiker, having expended the energy required to go there, uphill, no less, gets a pay-off in clear weather: a view. And because the view from the tower is unobstructed by trees, it is a 360-degree view. Many of the individual trail descriptions remind the hiker of that, so he or she may be encouraged to keep ascending. One does not receive such encouragement for many of the High Peaks. If you are having trouble getting up Cliff or Couchsachraga or Street, Nye, or Table Top Mountains, you have no incentive to keep going except for completion of your list. But here we have a list of peaks with juicy rewards.

Consider a few other reasons for choosing to climb these peaks. For one thing, they all have maintained trails. There are no herd paths to contend with. They are, for the most part, less crowded than the High Peaks, although Bald (Rondaxe), Blue, Hadley, and Goodnow Mountains attract a surprisingly large number of summer climbers. And because the trails are at lower elevations than those in the High Peaks, they lend themselves better to hardening against erosion and muddy puddles.

This is not to say that these hikes will give you less of a physical challenge than many of the forty-six High Peaks. For example, Snowy Mountain is a 2106-ft hike from the trailhead, and Gore Mountain is an ascent of 2533 ft. In the High Peaks, a climb of Cascade Mountain from the Cascade Lakes is only 1940 vertical feet, and Phelps Mountain is but 1982 ft above Heart Lake.

My hope, then, is that these descriptions, conveniently packaged together, may send those who have already climbed the forty-six High Peaks off to other choice summits tucked away in the far

Superlative Towers

There are lots of superlatives associated with fire towers. Some strictly factual ones follow, along the lines of the first, the highest, the farthest away... Try them on your friends.

1. Which fire tower is located highest in the Adirondacks?

2. Which tower is situated highest in the Catskills?

3. Which tower requires the longest hike?

4. Which tower has the shortest hike?

5. On which of these summits was the very first fire tower in all of New York State erected?

6. Which tower is the tallest?

7. Which tower summit requires the greatest ascent?

ANSWERS: 1. Snowy, elevation 3899 ft; 2. Hunter, elevation 4040 ft; 3. Woodhull, 7.6 mi one way; 4. Belfry, 0.3 mi, one way. (This summit has the best view for the hiker's energy expended.); 5. Balsam Lake Mountain, in 1887; 6. Spruce, at over 73 ft; 7. Gore, a 2533-ft climb corners of the Adirondack and Catskill Parks. And for those who have no use for compulsively climbing peaks on a list, but just want a pleasant day's outing, here are some choice selections.

If you're inclined to undertake a number of the hikes described in this book and record your observations, you'll want to know about ADK's Fire Tower Challenge. See page 142.

Wooden 40-ft observation platform built on Hunter Mountain in 1909. It was replaced by a steel Aermotor tower in 1917. The shed on the second landing, the subject of creative speculation in recent years, was probably only used to store tools. (Conservation Commission Annual Report)

A Room with a View:
A History of Fire Towers in the
Adirondacks and Catskills

The utilitarian steel fire tower has the aesthetic appeal of a can opener to some, while others see in it a skeletal obelisk or even a pantheistic spire. Yet few dispute its historic importance. No other structure has mattered so much in preserving the forests we enjoy today.

Once numbering more than 100, New York State's fire observation towers have performed several pivotal roles. In the often-contentious struggle among competing interests for the future of the forest, they provided a common ground to address threats to the forest as a resource. Their basic mission—preventing forest fires—was an unqualified success, yet their role in public education, if less noted, is equally impressive. In effect mountaintop classrooms, they schooled twentieth-century generations in modern conservation ethics.

Perhaps most important, these steel towers and their rustic predecessors shaped our perception of the forest in much the same way that the first photographs of Earth from space altered our parochial view of our planet. Towers enabled our forebears to literally see the forest through the trees, moving them to comprehend its vast scale, understand its importance, and dedicate themselves to its preservation.

The earliest mountaintop towers predated the establishment of New York State's Forest Preserve. In 1885 the Forest Commission Act placed all wild forest lands in the Adirondacks and Catskills under the supervision of a Forest Commission. This legislation represented the culmination of efforts by conservationists to curb abuses connected with lumbering, along with damage from forest fires, flooding, and other problems.

Protecting the state's forests from fire, whether they stood on public or private land, was a goal that all interested parties—loggers, sportsmen, and businessmen—agreed on. Once ignited, forest fires spread rapidly in dry years and were nearly impossible to extinguish. The logging practice of "topping" a harvested tree and leaving the highly flammable slash behind on the forest floor created a serious hazard. Prominent among the major agents of ignition were farmers and berry pickers, who burned over hayfields and meadows to improve yields; iron manufacturers; collectors of

This 18-ft Gore Mountain observation platform constructed in 1909 was replaced 9 years later by a 60-ft Aermotor tower. Could this observer envision the future of such observation stations or their steel replacements? (Conservation Commission Annual Report)

tree gum and bees; hunters; and vandals. In the 1890s, when railroads reached into the Adirondack interior, sparks from locomotive stacks and brakes, and live coals from fireboxes, joined this list.

New York State gradually responded to these threats by developing a fire observation network. The system evolved in three distinct phases. The earliest days (1870–1908) saw short-lived wooden towers erected for other purposes on mountain summits appropriated as outlooks for fires. These were followed, in the 1909–1915 era, by more substantial purpose-built fire observation towers that were staffed during the summer and connected by telephone to settlements in the valleys below. Encouraged by the success of this network, and in response to increased tourist activity generated by automobile travel, the system enjoyed an expansionist third phase, from 1916 to World War II. During this period, the state added new stations and replaced earlier ones with taller, standardized steel towers that were better suited to weathering the severe summit climates and accommodating increasing numbers of recreational visitors.

Fledgling Efforts (1870–1908)

In New York, the first elevated platforms on mountain summits were built as scenic overlooks by the private sector in and near the Catskill region. Perhaps the earliest tower of this sort was an octagonal 20-foot wooden structure built around 1870 by Albert and Alfred Smiley on a height near Mohonk Lake on the Shawangunk ridge. It provided guests at the family's resort with grand vistas over what would soon become part of the Forest Preserve. Another, less typical example was the enclosed four-stage observatory built on Mount Utsayantha, near Stamford, by Colonel Rulif W. Rulifson in 1882.

The first towers built by the state were signal stations for Verplanck Colvin's survey of the Adirondack wilderness, begun in 1872. Colvin's crews built temporary towers on various summits in order to gauge mountain heights. Typically, these structures employed four stout poles set at an inwardly inclined taper and trussed with cross braces of thinner poles. In many cases the towers opened up views previously obscured by trees. One such was the signal station built on Blue Mountain in 1873, which became a tourist destination after the surveyors departed. By the end of the 1870s, the survey tower was helping shape the public's attitude toward the forest, as this passage from A. Judd Northrup's *Camps and Tramps in the Adirondacks* (1880) attests:

> . . . we came to a "timber slash" of ten or fifteen acres, where the trees had been felled to give an unobstructed view in every direction. In the midst of this opening, founded upon primeval rock which bears the surveyor's cabalistic characters ineradicably sunk into the solid mass, is erected a tall, steeple-like skeleton structure of strongly-braced timbers, on the top of which is fastened the signal of bright tin, which can be seen flashing in the sun many miles away, from valley and mountain peak. . . . Upon these timbers we climbed, and perching there, twenty feet from the rocks beneath, gazed in

every direction upon a wonderful scene. Until then we had never properly conceived of the grandeur of this remarkable region, nor the "general plan," of the mountains, lakes and rivers of the Adirondack wilderness. It is forest every where, and mountain, lake and river repeated on every hand; and all these are seen, I imagine, with something of the effect produced upon the mind of the beholder by looking down upon these features of nature from a balloon.

Not all early towers were devoted to science or recreation. Some supplemented the state's nascent fire protection program. The Forest Commission's system, launched in 1885, consisted of appointing a fire warden for each town in the Forest Preserve. Actual fire prevention, however, was limited to posting the commission's fire regulations at the edges of the forest. No provision was made for preventive surveillance, even in times of drought, when it was most needed. Instead, the program emphasized "extinction." The warden was directed to raise and supervise firefighting crews, but although the state appointed wardens, the towns were expected to pay for their services and the costs of fire suppression. Wardens worked only during emergencies, and often had trouble raising crews because men doubted that the towns would in fact compensate them.

The young program was not only structurally flawed; it also failed to effectively address two major causes of fires: the increasing presence of railroads penetrating Adirondack forests, and the illegal burning of wild blueberry fields in the Catskills. Some owners of private preserves, such as Nehasane's William Seward Webb, purchased their own firefighting equipment, established fire roads, and maintained crews to remove slash and patrol railroad rights-of-way. Other private preserves and resorts erected observation towers from which illegal burning could be spotted. The first such documented structure in New York was built in 1887 by the Balsam Lake Club, a private fishing organization, atop Balsam Lake Mountain, about 15 miles south of Arkville in western Ulster County. The tower was built of logs cut near the summit and staffed by a spotter during periods of drought.

The effectiveness of surveillance was demonstrated during the dry summer of 1899, when some 322 fires burned more than 79,653 acres in the state. Although roughly a third of the Adirondack forest was owned by private clubs or held as private preserves, not one fire occurred on these lands because they were thoroughly and efficiently guarded. Well aware of this discrepancy, the Forest Commission proposed establishing a force of patrolling forest rangers, but the notion was not acted on.

The first decade of the twentieth century remained exceptionally dry in the Northeast. In late spring and early summer of 1903, 643 fires burned approximately 428,180 acres in the Adirondacks and more than 36,000 acres in the Catskills. The principal agents of fire were the logging operations that followed the railroads into the Adirondacks. While private preserves fared better than public lands, there were substantial losses in both sectors. Fire claimed 40,000 acres of the Rockefeller preserve near Santa Clara, 12,000 acres of Webb's Nehasane, 10,000 acres of property owned by A.A. Low near Horseshoe Lake, 5,000 acres of the Whitney preserve, 2,000 acres at the Brandreth preserve, and Henry van Hoevenberg's Adirondack Lodge (later Adirondak Loj) near Lake Placid. The press deemed the Rockefeller blaze suspicious and blamed it on "incindieries and degenerates" angered over the forced resettlement of the hamlet of Brandon. Between 1904 and 1908 some 1,172 fires burned an additional 393,647 acres in the Catskill and Adirondack State Parks.

Fires during the drought of 1908 were unusually severe, with smoke shrouding much of the Northeast through the summer. The annual visitation of fires imparted a sense of disorientation, terror, helplessness, and resignation on many residents and visitors to the mountains as attested by this letter to *Forest and Stream* on October 17 from a Blue Mountain Lake resident:

> A few weeks ago smoke was observed—where did it come from? Some said Minnesota, others Michigan, still others said there must be a fire somewhere in our own forests. Day by day the smoke increased, and then news came of several Adirondack fires. Still little was thought of it. But the smoke increased, the air became heavy, tainted, vitiated, its vitality burned up, and the heat correspondingly increased. Even the sun was partially obscured, and all nature trembled, as if awaiting a catastrophe. Physical depression resulted; in many cases it became mental. The fires were all around—spreading, approaching. Some hamlets were destroyed. This was not reassuring. The fires increased in number, they were coming nearer. Men felt their inability to cope with them. Non-religious men said, "We ought to pray for rain." Some did it. On Sept. 28 it came; moderately during the afternoon—more at night. People smiled as they met. Some sang the Doxology. The fires could now be controlled, the air was clearer, the long strain was over.

A State System Evolves (1909–1916)

The climate of crisis that lingered on in the early twentieth century prompted private landowners to upgrade or add preventative fire observation measures and stimulated the state to attack the problem. Sweeping amendments to the Forest, Fish and Game law were enacted in the spring of 1909 that shifted the major operating expenses for fire protection from the towns to the state and provided for a more extensive program organized by fire districts (initially three in the Adirondacks and one in the Catskills).

Each district was administered by a trained superintendent who supervised a force of rangers or patrolmen charged with prevention and early response. District superintendents were also directed to establish a network of mountaintop fire observation towers staffed seasonally by trained spotters and connected by telephone to headquarters. In addition, the legislation empowered the governor to close forests to the public during periods of drought and mandated new regulations for railroads and logging operations, including preventive appliances on locomotives, removal of slash near railbeds, and a ban on top-lopping.

In revamping its program, the Forest, Fish and Game Commission incorporated successful measures used in private preserves and other states. New York adopted its system of observation towers from a program in Maine, which had proved successful in limiting losses in 1908 compared to those sustained in other forested states. Maine's forest commissioner, Edgar R. Ring, described the system to New York officials thus:

> They are connected by telephone to the nearest firewarden and are equipped with a range finder, compass, strong field glasses, and a plan of the surrounding country, drawn to a careful scale. With these instruments, our wardens have located fires accurately 30 miles distant, notified the wardens and had them extinguished before making any great headway. The cost of installing these stations of course depends upon the length of telephone line, but we have estimated that the stations in this State cost from $400 to $800. . . . In my opinion one man located at a station will do more effectual work in discovering and locating fires than a hundred would do patrolling. Of course patrols are needed to follow up on camping parties, and with a good system of lookout stations and patrols you have got a system for fire protection which is pretty near the thing.

The commission quickly embraced the Maine program. By the end of 1909 five fire observation stations were operational, and an additional six would be ready for use the following year. Four more would soon be in the works.

The most labor-intensive task in establishing the stations was running roughly 73 miles of telephone line through difficult terrain. The lines were connected to main lines where possible, but in some cases the state was forced to buy private lines. Once in place, the communications system linked far-flung stations with district headquarters in Lake Placid, Northville, Old Forge, and Seager; with regional ranger stations in nearby towns; and with fire crews on private preserves.

During the early years, observers located fires using the first editions of USGS topographical maps where available. These were positioned on a table at the summit and oriented to the surrounding countryside. By 1913 alidades and, where practicable, range finders were in use.

The immediate success of the program in controlling forest fires in 1909 and 1910 cleared the way for expansion. In 1910 the Forest, Fish and Game Commission noted:

> The value of the observation stations has been fully demonstrated. . . . The former method, waiting until smoke from a fire was so voluminous that it attracted attention several miles away, is too precarious and causes not only great property losses, but forest destruction. . . . The "smokes" are now observed when the fires are in their incipiency. . . . The cost of construction and maintenance is nothing in comparison with the property saved, forest protected and reduction in the cost of forest fires. The number of stations should be increased to at least thirty.

The size of the network increased steadily, to 20 stations in 1910, 36 in 1911, and 49 in 1912. Early detection was clearly working. Between 1909 and 1913, some 2,251 fires damaged 124,134 acres. Compared with the preceding five-year period, the average amount of acreage damaged had been reduced from 335 acres to 55 per fire, and the average monetary damage per acre had fallen from $712 to $65.

Due to limited appropriations, stations built during this period of rapid expansion were temporary and inexpensive. Structural configurations varied widely. Towers and platforms were built only where needed (seven of the twenty stations placed in service in the first 2 years had sufficient sightlines to require none). Nearly all the early towers were built of wood. At least one, the tower on Prospect Mountain near Lake George Village, had been recycled.

A former hotel cupola, it was hauled intact to the summit. An un-usual three-level tower on Hunter Mountain, at 40 feet among the tallest of the group, was built with three plumb log or stump legs braced by triangular pole trusses. The one on Makomis Mountain was also distinctive, faced with clapboards from the ground up, with an enclosed cab beneath a gable roof.

More typical were open, rustic towers apparently informed by steel versions, with four inwardly angled log legs cross-braced by poles. Others appear to have been built in haste or based on non-traditional forms, such as the horizontally braced towers at Hamilton Mountain and Mount Adams. With few exceptions, observers stood in the open on wood platforms. Only two towers of this generation were built of steel: those at Belleayre Mountain and Twadell Point. Both were standard windmill towers built with angle-iron legs and terminating in open platforms.

In 1913 and 1914 the Conservation Commission, successor to the Forest, Fish and Game Commission, replaced eight of this first generation of towers. Some replacements appear to have used tall standing tree stumps growing closely together as uprights, with the tops cut off and a platform of poles laid on top.

Initially, observers camped in tents or primitive huts at or near their stations, but as the commission noted, "A substantial cabin is much to be preferred, as the weather conditions on the top of the mountain are often rigorous, even during the summer months." By the close of the 1912 season, thirty-two of the stations had cabins, of which twenty-two were built of logs and the rest framed with lumber. Like the towers themselves, the cabins varied in size, shape, and claddings, which included shingles, clapboard, and bark. Telephone equipment was housed in cabinets mounted on the towers or freestanding shanties.

Expansion (1916–1945)

The final phase of fire tower development resulted from the state's efforts to combine fire protection with recreation management. Between 1916 and 1920, the renamed Conservation Commission improved trail access to its fire observation stations and replaced the first generation of temporary towers with more durable steel structures able to accommodate public use.

Recreational use of the forest had long been a subject of discussion, even prior to the establishment of the Forest Preserve in 1885. Since the 1870s, public recreation and commercial logging had been seen as competing and mutually exclusive interests. Through the first decade of the twentieth century, the state limited its forest

Lumber slash left along an Adirondack railroad in Franklin County. Such practices early in the 1900s led to disastrous fires that burned a million acres in 1903 and 1908.

management role to conservation, leaving development of infrastructures for logging and recreation to the private sector on private land.

Increasing demand for recreational camping prompted a change in policy. By the early twentieth century the State of New York had become the largest forest landowner in the eastern United States, with vast tracts of wilderness within reach of the country's major population centers. Railroads controlled the flow and limited the destination of these urban visitors through the turn of the century. The automobile would soon make the Preserve accessible at many more points to greater numbers of visitors than ever before.

Recreational activities had been concentrated around resort hotels and clubs accessible by public transportation. Forays into the forest were typically led by local guides who knew the terrain and the importance of fire safety. With the advent of the automobile, wilderness became accessible to the general public. As the guiding profession declined, the number of fires rose. In 1914 fires caused by fishermen, hunters, and campers exceeded 50 percent of all fires, 44 percent of the land damaged, and 57 percent of the total monetary loss.

In an effort to address the problem, in 1913 the Conservation

Commission began permitting private individuals, associations, and corporations to construct lean-tos on state lands, with the stipulation that they be posted as property of the State of New York, open to the public, and equipped with safe fireplaces.

The commission's attitude toward the public had become somewhat ambivalent, alternately scolding and begrudging. Its stance was ineffective in controlling fires and actually worked against its best interests by alienating its base of support: the people of the state.

In 1915 the agency was reorganized under Commissioner George DuPont Pratt, an officer of the Standard Oil Company, president of the Pratt Institute, an avid sportsman, and a former president of the Camp Fire Club of America. (He would later become the first president of the Adirondack Mountain Club.) Under his leadership the commission came to understand the importance of public support in justifying its conservation work and expanding the Forest Preserve. In his preamble to the commission's 1915 report, Pratt reached out to the preserve's natural constituency and spelled out a fresh vision for the agency, broadening the definition of conservation and equating it with the public good:

> . . . it must not be forgotten that conservation has a less tangible, but none the less real, basis of justification. Conservation deals with those things to which practically every normal person turns for relaxation in his moments of leisure. It deals among other things, with the forests, for which an innate love has been implanted in every man. . . . The Commission desires here to emphasize its belief in the tremendous importance of the aesthetic and recreational advantage derived from conservation, no less than the financial returns that are more easily traced. It has no data on which to base an estimate of the number of people who annually spend their vacations in the forest counties. But none are needed, for the part which those wooded sections play in the pleasure and health of the people of the State is evident to all who consider it. . . . Comment is made on another page of the number of forest, fish and game associations and similar organizations in the State whose reason for existence is almost entirely the protection of our forests and wild life. Through all of these organizations runs the spirit of social service. Their conduct entails much work and sacrifice upon their officers and guiding minds. That this work is faithfully and consistently performed and supported as universally as it is, is but another proof of the social value of conservation—proof that places it on a plane with education, child welfare work, the labor

movement, the various campaigns for public health, and every other activity for social betterment.

Drawing on his skills as a businessman, educator, and outdoorsman, Pratt managed and promoted recreational use of the Forest Preserve while strengthening the fire protection system. The foundation of the program was an innovative grassroots public education campaign launched in 1915 to reach the principal cause of fires—smokers, fishermen, hunters, campers, and youngsters who would soon undertake these activities. The new campaign distributed fire protection posters and postcards throughout the state's railway system and public schools.

Perhaps the most farsighted vehicle was a movie, *The Match in the Forest*. Apparently filmed by Pratt himself, the silent film followed the course of a fire from ignition to detection by an observer at his tower to the response of firefighters bringing it under control. The film, accompanied by lectures illustrated with stereopticon slides, traveled statewide to forest organizations, fish and game associations, granges, YMCAs, churches, and other groups.

Tied in with the education campaign was a concerted effort to upgrade the observation stations, now made famous by the film, to accommodate the public. Between 1916 and 1920 the commission replaced earlier stations and erected new ones with prefabricated steel windmill structures. The derrick-like trussed steel tower was the newly emerging standard in federal and state forests. They were purchased from the Aermotor Company, a leading manufacturer of self-oiling windmills based in Chicago (see sidebar, p. 31). By 1920 there were fifty new towers in service.

The upgrading program also included replacing the first generation of staff housing. The new cabins were more comfortable for the observers and more presentable to the public, but were not yet standardized. The one at Ampersand, for example, was a simple log cabin with saddle-notch corners and a detached log lean-to. At the same time, public accessibility to the observation stations was made a priority. Uniform "guideboards" depicting routes to the summits were placed at trailheads, and the towers purchased in 1916 were retrofitted with stairs for public use. Education became part of the observers' mission. Staff were trained to teach visitors about fire safety and demonstrate their equipment.

An Osborne Fire Finder, developed by the U.S. Forest Service, was installed on a test basis at Poke-O-Moonshine Mountain in 1918. It was a customized panoramic map of the territory that duplicated what was visible to the observer. Covered with a heavy glass plate and equipped with a hole at the center to accommodate an alidade, the apparatus helped pinpoint fires more accurately than topographic maps. It also proved to be of significant interest to visitors. Similar maps were subsequently prepared for each station. Visitorship increased through the decades prior to World War II, from 30,500 in 1921 to 55,500 in 1930 and peaking at nearly 91,000 in 1941. Camping was encouraged at sites adjacent to the trails.

The observers were indispensable to the success of the program: they embodied the spirit of the Adirondack guide and put a face on the agency. In addition to their spotting responsibilities, they served as educators, naturalists, and folklorists. The also performed many other tasks: maintaining trails and telephone lines, performing search-and-rescue operations, and occasionally firefighting.

Since observers were on duty throughout the fire season, comfortable quarters were deemed essential to the efficient operation of the stations. The first "standard" observers' cabins, resembling the three-room arrangement in use through the 1960s, were built in 1927, and more soon followed. Many of the observers of this period were committed to their work, and domesticated the grounds around their cabins with vegetable cellars, apple trees, and outbuildings for storing wood and perishables.

Further growth and improvements came during the Depression of the 1930s, largely through the efforts of the federal Civilian Conservation Corps (CCC). The CCC "camps" that sprang up across the state were responsible for work projects including fire fighting, reforestation, and construction of fire towers and fire truck trails. Under the CCC, access trails to many observation stations were built or improved with new culverts and retaining walls. Bridges and many cabins were rebuilt or replaced. The CCC also extended the height of the tower at Snowy Mountain by adding a stage at its base, and undertook most of the maintenance of telephone lines from 1933 to 1937.

By the end of the decade 2.4 million acres of forestland were under the Conservation Department's oversight. Within this department, the Bureau of Forest Fire Protection included 87 forest rangers, 13 district rangers, and 84 fire observers and observation stations.

Decline and Rebirth (1945–2000)

World War II brought change to the system, which signaled the end of the fire towers' usefulness. The Conservation Department dealt with funding cutbacks during the war years by closing all but the most critical stations and investigating less labor-intensive means of surveillance.

Wind, Water, and Fire

Prefabricated steel towers were introduced on a large scale to the American public in the 1890s at expositions and state fairs. Their original purpose was to carry windmills used to pump water from wells, and they became common features in the parched West on farmsteads and at railroad fueling stations.

The windmill towers of the Aermotor Company adapted easily to use as fire observation posts in the large forest of the northeast United States. The upper tapered stages that supported the windmill were replaced by an enclosed steel cab approximately 7 feet square. Heights were adjusted by adding increasingly larger standard truss sections to the bottom. In a three-stage tower, the most common type used in New York State, the floor of the cab was 33 feet above the ground. Fourth, fifth, and sixth stages extended cab height to 45 feet 9 inches, 59 feet 3 inches, and 79 feet 6 inches, respectively.

Models with varying gauges of steel and special connections were tailored to different wind and ground conditions. At the base, angle-iron legs were held by patented foot clamps. These were anchored directly to the exposed ledge by countersunk rods, where possible, and most often leveled by raised concrete piers. Many towers were further anchored with guys. The structures ordered in 1916 were designed for use without stairs; later towers incorporated heavier members to accommodate the added weight of steel staircases with wood treads.

Hefting several tons of steel components to the summits was difficult. In most cases it could not be accomplished by motorized vehicles alone. At Mount Adams in Essex County, for example, the components were brought partway from the base of the mountain over a corduroy road. At road's end they were off-loaded and skidded some distance by a team of horses, then carried by hand up the final pitch by rangers, foresters, and observers.

Although the towers were designed either to be assembled on the ground and then raised, or constructed in place piece by piece, the ledge and rugged terrain at the summits precluded the former method. Typically, the foot clamps were set in anchor holes drilled into the granite or into poured-in-place concrete pads. The leg, stair, and strut sections were then lifted and bolted in place, and the observation cab assembled on top.

—W.H.H.

The seeds had been sown several years earlier. The department had purchased its first aircraft, a Fleet biplane, in 1931 to assist in fire monitoring. Tests of radio communication between the airplane and the State Office Building in Albany were conducted in 1937, and in 1941 the department announced that the radiophone had outgrown the experimental stage. During the war its use in fire spotting compensated for labor shortages. After the war, as the first generation of observers retired, the department had trouble finding the labor to rehabilitate its fire towers, observers' cabins, telephone circuits, and trails, even though this work had been approved by the Public Works Planning Commission. The postwar period also witnessed the gradual transition from telephone to radio communication between the towers and their bases, and an increasing reliance on aerial surveillance. Nothing, however, replaced the observers' educational mission.

In 1971, New York State adopted an aerial fire surveillance program, and 61 of the 102 towers were closed by the Bureau of Forest Fire Control. Strategic stations were staffed during seasons of extreme hazard, but most were abandoned and left exposed to the elements. The reclassification of Forest Preserve lands undertaken by the Department of Environmental Conservation (DEC) in the 1980s led the agency responsible for their care to declare deteriorated structures on wild lands attractive nuisances and schedule their removal. When it became evident that the towers enjoyed strong popular support, however, the removal project was deferred. Then, during the weekend of April 18–19, 1992, the decommissioned tower on Pharaoh Mountain in Essex County was toppled by a vandal and removed by DEC helicopter. The Pharaoh tower became a symbol: the crime was seen by some as an attack on the Forest Preserve itself.

The ensuing public outrage galvanized a grassroots response by an assortment of organizations, public and private, whose members found new and unprecedented common ground in the plight of the towers. The consortium included the Adirondack Mountain Club, the Catskill Center, Adirondack Architectural Heritage, extension agencies, county and town governments, friends' groups, pulp companies, property rights advocates, and sympathetic DEC employees.

A strategy for preserving the towers through adoption by friends' groups has emerged from this effort. The state now permits these groups to stabilize and repair the towers to DEC engineering specifications, with the understanding that they will maintain and operate the stations seasonally for educational purposes. This model program has been implemented on the summits of Arab,

Azure, Bald (Rondaxe), Blue, Cathedral Rock, Goodnow, Hadley, Kane, Owls Head, Poke-O-Moonshine, and Vanderwhacker in the Adirondacks, and on Balsam Lake, Hunter, Overlook, Red Hill, and Tremper in the Catskills.

Another recent trend has been use of the stations as radio and cellular communications facilities. Several have been adapted by state police as radio repeater towers. Equipment attached to the towers or at their bases may seem unsightly, but at the same time the work has included much-needed repairs to correct problems of neglect and extend the structures' service life. One can hope that these towers will survive the next revolution in communications technology.

These landmarks remind us how fragile the Adirondack and Catskill forests are and how close we came to losing them. What better means is there to pass this lesson along, one generation to the next, than the towers themselves? Their preservation is in the public interest, and the recent listing of ten of the remaining towers on the State and National Register of Historic Places signals a positive attitudinal shift by the public and the public agencies charged with their care.

Nonetheless, their future remains cloudy. The register, for example, puts in place procedural controls to encourage preservation of the listed towers, but does not itself mandate or fund any maintenance and repair. Repair needs are extensive after years of neglect and exposure to the elements. Wooden steps and cab

The advent of light aircraft for monitoring in the 1930s offered easier and cheaper fire detection in remote parts of New York State forests .

decks are gone, windows are missing, connections are rusted because of lack of paint, and the steel itself shows signs of fatigue in some exposed locations. Once these are remedied, the question of how the towers will be maintained and renewed over the long haul needs to be answered.

It is in the interest of the state to commemorate its stunning accomplishment in conserving the forest resource by preserving the towers. More importantly, it is in the interest of all who benefit from the forest to safeguard its future by remembering its past.

Wesley H. Haynes
Hebron, New York
March 8, 2001

Research for this essay was supported by a grant to the Adirondack Architectural Heritage from the New York State Council on the Arts, a state agency, and the Preservation League of New York State.

How to Use This Book

Each hike description in this guidebook begins with summary information that will enable you to estimate the difficulty of the trail. Distances and elevation change data will help you determine if the trips are within your capability. If you have scant prior hiking experience, you may want to compare this info with that of another hike you've completed. The combined effect of distance and elevation change is worth noting too; you may find a short hike challenging if the elevation change is significant.

The difficulty ratings are necessarily subjective. What is steep to one person may be easy to another. No two people seem to evaluate trail difficulty in the same manner. I have attempted to standardize the use of terms relating to steepness in the trail summaries. Four terms are used: easy, moderate, strenuous, and difficult. Appendix B, Comparison of Route Difficulty, should assist you in choosing hikes and in evaluating your experience of a particular trail relative to the book's trail ratings overall.

Page-Map Legend

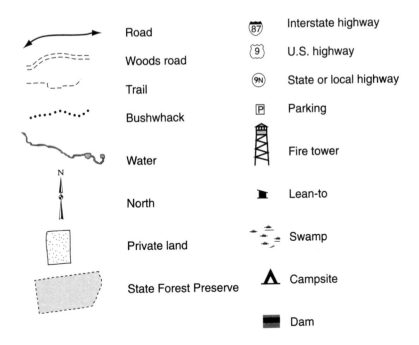

Road	Interstate highway ⑧⑦
Woods road	U.S. highway ⑨
Trail	State or local highway ⑨ⓝ
Bushwhack	Parking 🅿
Water	Fire tower
North	Lean-to
Private land	Swamp
State Forest Preserve	Campsite
	Dam

A Few Words about Maps

General overview maps of the Adirondack and Catskill Parks and their respective fire towers follow the Contents list. In addition, each fire tower trail has an accompanying page map, a legend for which is printed on page 35. For those who wish to obtain more detailed maps, the summary information will assist you.

For the Adirondack trails, the map references listed at the beginning of each route description refer to one of the seven large maps that accompany the seven volumes of ADK's *Guide to Adirondack Trails*. These maps may be purchased separately from the volumes. For the Catskill trails, the map references are to one of four Catskill trail maps, Numbers 41–44, published by the New York–New Jersey Trail Conference. All of these maps are available from the Adirondack Mountain Club (1-800-395-8080, 8:30 A.M.– 5 P.M., M–Sat.). See the publications list in the back of this volume.

Each route description also lists the pertinent topographical quadrangle from the United States Geological Survey (USGS). An index for New York State and an order form are available by writing USGS Information Services, Box 25286, Denver, Colorado 80225 (telephone: 1-800-ASK-USGS; fax: 303-202-4693) or on the Internet at the USGS Web site: <www.usgs.gov/>.

Trail Habits and Practices

What Do You Need?
The beginning hiker is often bewildered by the wide assortment of equipment available on the market today. Don't let this discourage you. Day hikes are not lengthy expeditions, and while equipment should be sturdy and dependable, it doesn't have to be expensive. Though there are factors that should be addressed before setting out on a hike, they are relatively few: comfort, adaptability to changing conditions, health, safety, and personal interests. Most people find they already have several of the items needed for hiking. Don't be distracted by today's sophisticated marketing of outdoor equipment; for now purchase only those supplies that satisfy your needs.

Comfort
Your feet are going to get you there, so treat them kindly. Generally the steeper the trail or the heavier the hiker, the more rugged the footwear. Acceptable footwear should fit well, be sturdy, provide ankle support, and have good traction. Shoes or boots should be well broken-in. For most of the hikes in this book, sneakers or work shoes are adequate. Light or medium-weight hiking boots serve better, however, and often provide additional ankle support. Sneakers may be fine on a short, flat, dry trail, but they can become mighty uncomfortable on a muddy mountain trail that floods during an unexpected deluge. Many hikers wear an outer pair of heavy woolen socks and a lighter pair of socks underneath them to reduce friction. Rest occasionally so your feet can cool off—or they may present you with a blister to remind you to be more concerned with their welfare.

In everyday life most of us don't think much about walking. We get up from the the table and walk to the living room or car. The act is over after a dozen or so steps. Hiking is considerably different. Besides having proper footwear, it helps a great deal to have your hands free. You don't mind carrying a picnic basket from the kitchen to the car, but don't try to carry one five miles up a mountain.

Put your food, sweater, and other gear in a pack of some sort. For a short trip this may be a travel bag over the shoulder or a fanny pack. Eventually, however, you'll want a day pack. The cost, quality, and type depends upon your needs and your body build. Size can only be determined after you know what must be carried. Late fall and winter hiking require extra space for supplemental clothing. Many packs are compressible so size can be altered. Generally, soft packs rather than external frame packs are more comfortable for day hikes. Some light internal frame packs are also excellent. Fifteen or twenty pounds are as much as a person can easily tote all day. Carry less if possible. Make sure the pack stitching is good and that stress points are double-stitched. Try on several styles to find which type feels most comfortable on your back. An occasional hiker doesn't need the same quality gear as the every-weekend hiker whose gear will get more wear and tear. Cost generally varies with quality.

Adaptability to changing conditions

Anyone who has spent time in the Adirondacks has heard the old adage, "If you don't like the weather, wait around ten minutes and it'll change." Even when the weather doesn't change, the hiker will find it cooler in the forest than out in the sunny meadow. The temperature drops and winds increase as you gain elevation. On the driest of days you'll still get soaked if you slip while crossing a stream. It is only good sense to prepare for the likely, but it is prudent to prepare for the unlikely as well.

One of the most simple, practical items for adaptability is a hat. It protects you from sun, rain, and insects. Wet, it will help cool you on a hot day. In the rain, its brim is a blessing. (Put some insect repellent around the brim and watch those pesky flies disappear.) In cooler weather a wool cap will keep you warm even when wet. Up to a third of your body heat can be controlled through your head. Getting warm after climbing awhile? Take your hat off. Getting cold? Put one on.

Make your equipment serve many functions. You can use a poncho to help keep you warm, protect you from the wind, and stay dry in the rain. Those extra socks you were wise enough to carry make pretty good mittens on a chilly day. A hood is desirable on that poncho or jacket. *The key to heat control is layering. Avoid perspiration.* Start with that light jacket or wool shirt you have in the closet. Consider the number of combinations a wool or synthetic vest and rain jacket can offer. Carry items that can be taken off or added easily and make the adjustment as soon as your body indicates a change is needed. That heavy parka may be great for sitting in a cold stadium, but don't try to climb a mountain in it.

One more word is needed: *hypothermia.* This is a condition in which heat loss exceeds the body's ability to replace heat. Core body temperature decreases, and death can result.

The air temperature need not be frigid for this to happen. Even on a sunny summer day a high wind can strip body heat away quickly. Avoid cotton clothes, which wick water and cause body heat loss. Use synthetics in the summer and wool outer layers with synthetic long underwear in the winter. Avoid soaking your clothing with perspiration. Remember the concept of clothing layering.

Should you or a companion find that you are losing gloves or other clothing items on the trail, stumbling while walking, experiencing uncontrollable shivering, having difficulty thinking, or responding oddly to queries, act without delay. Get hot food and drink into the person, favoring high-energy, quickly digested foods. Get the person warmed in any manner possible. All hikers should familiarize themselves with the symptoms of hypothermia and the remedial actions necessary to prevent it.

Health

Get a good night's rest before setting out on your trip. Follow up with a good, high-energy breakfast so you'll maintain your stamina after a few hours of walking. Many hikers prefer to nibble food throughout the day rather than have a single large midday meal. Hard candies, nuts, raisins and other dried fruits, sunflower seeds, granola, coconut, dried cereal, chocolate, and other readily available supermarket items make good trail food ("gorp"). Semisweet chocolate won't melt in hot weather. A fresh orange is great to have along. On day trips, avoid lunch foods that require cooking; this saves time and spares you carrying cooking gear.

You should drink more water than usual when you hike. Take a filled plastic water bottle with you. (Unfortunately, no water source on or off the trail can be considered safe to drink owing to the prevalence of the parasite *Giardia lamblia*. Carry water purification tablets or a water filter in case of emergency.) Carry extra food, and bring those wrappers and containers out with you.

It is often said that God's only mistake was creating the black fly. Spring hiking calls for a suitable insect repellent. The most effective ones have the active ingredient N, N-diethyl-meta-toluamide (DEET). (For children, choose a repellent *without* DEET, however.) By mid-July you may be tempted to leave repellents at home, but don't do it. It's a small item to carry for the relief it provides when you need it.

Carry a first aid kit containing an assortment of Band Aids, salves, small bandages, a small pair of scissors, and, in extremely warm weather, salt tablets. An Ace bandage is nice to have for a turned ankle. An antihistamine may be useful for a chance insect sting.

If you feel a tender spot developing on your foot, care for it immediately before it becomes a blister. Moleskin patches are handy for this. Cut a small hole in the center of the patch a little larger than the sore spot. Place the patch on the skin with the hole over the tender spot. The raised patch then keeps the boot from irritating it more.

Don't forget toilet tissue and a small, light trowel. Although many hiking areas have privies at campsites along the trails, don't count on one being present when you need it. Leave the trail, select an area of soft earth, and make a small hole 6–8 inches deep. Cover it with leaf litter before leaving it. Nature will take care of the rest. Be sure to avoid areas near waterways.

Safety

Be conservative in estimating the time you will need for a hike—and don't forget to factor in your return. Some people walk faster than others, and even the same person may push on rapidly when a storm beckons overhead but tarry while observing wildflowers on a warm spring day. Are you in good physical condition? Do you have a small child along with you who may have to be carried from time to time? These are variables that must be considered.

Caution

When considering climbing a fire tower, rely on your own judgement, bearing in mind that you climb these towers at your own risk. Windy, stormy weather makes the climbing of even restored towers risky.

Trail descriptions in this book lead to several towers that either are not open to the public or are in a state of disrepair. If the DEC has closed a tower to the public, it is for good reason. Respect their decision.

Consult your watch, noting the approximate midpoint of the time you had planned to be hiking—and turn around a little before then, even if you haven't reached your destination. This can make the difference between a good experience and an unpleasant, if not dangerous, conclusion to your hike, especially when bad weather or dusk is approaching. After a trip or two you should be able to compare the travel times of past outings and estimate accordingly in planning future hikes.

Remember that trail conditions vary through time. Rains make some areas very slippery. Spring meltwaters can wash out bridges and make normally small streams uncrossable torrents.

While Forest Preserve trails are generally in good repair, funding for trail maintenance is often in short supply. It benefits hikers to use common sense and reasonable precautions if they encounter unusual conditions.

Emergencies do occur, but their intensity may be minimized if you are prepared for them. A few basic items can make the difference between inconvenience and disaster. Do not expect someone to appear simply because you need help. Even if you were sensible enough to tell a neighbor or friend of your intended route of travel and your expected return time, help should not be expected for several hours.

Although it may appear difficult to become lost on these trails, carry your guidebook anyway. Its page maps and text can help you gain insight about your trip. If you have a topographical map, orient yourself and identify points of interest that are in view.

The trails in this guide are, for the most part, well marked, but you should always carry a compass. Check your compass direction at the outset so you'll know which way to head should you become temporarily "misplaced." Take the time to become familiar with your compass *before* you need it.

Be sure to take plenty of dry matches. A candle greatly facilitates starting a fire in wet weather. If a fire is needed, build it on a rock base to prevent starting a ground fire in organic duff.

Every person in your group should carry a whistle. A lost child can panic. Teach him or her to sit down and use that whistle if separated from the party. The whistle can also be used to scare away a menacing animal. This is much safer than throwing things at it, which might cause it to attack you.

Time passes quickly when you're enjoying yourself. For added protection against a return trip in the dark, carry a flashlight or headlamp and allow ample time to be off the trail before nightfall.

A pocket knife has a multitude of uses. Don't wear a large jack knife unless you're planning to skin a buffalo. A small pocket knife with a couple of different-sized blades will fit the bill.

Many hikers carry a space blanket. They are light, small, and can be very useful if you get caught out overnight. They can be extremely important if a person is seriously injured and must be kept warm.

Don't fill your pockets with all these little items; walking will be most unpleasant. Instead, make or buy a ditty bag and attach a drawstring to close it. Throw all the loose items into the little sack and place it in the bottom of your pack. You'll know where everything is, and packing becomes a cinch.

Personal interests

Plan to enjoy yourself. What do you like to do? Take a camera if you like photography. A field identification guide to flowers, trees, birds, or animal tracks can make your trip more fun. A small pair of binoculars can improve the view or help you spot distant wildlife. Maybe you would just like to read a novel and while away the time. Whatever it is, tuck it into your pack and have a good time.

Trail Manners

Remember that you are a visitor in a place of natural beauty and it is likely others will follow in your steps. "Take only pictures, leave only footprints," is an excellent motto to follow. Many hikers habitually carry litter bags and clear trails as they return after a trip. There are other signs as well indicating that hikers are becoming more aware of their personal obligation to maintain the natural surroundings. Set a good example.

Campfires

The growing Leave-No-Trace ethic suggests that open fires should not be built in the wild except in those areas specifically established for that purpose. Lean-tos normally have fire rings, as do certain camping areas. Remember that Forest Preserve land is to be "forever wild." This means that no standing trees may be legally cut. Use dead and down wood only. Although you may enjoy a campfire at night, you'll find that camp cooking will be cleaner, faster, and can be done safely in more locations if a small portable camper's stove is carried with you on overnight trips.

Checklist of Hiking Equipment

☐ Map	☐ Jacket with hood
☐ Guidebook	☐ Poncho or other rain gear
☐ Water bottle, plastic	☐ Extra socks
☐ Flashlight or headlamp	☐ Whistle
☐ Matches	☐ Space blanket
☐ First aid kit	☐ Personal interest items
☐ Water purification tablets	☐ Day pack
☐ Compass	☐ Food and water
☐ Pocket knife	☐ Candle
☐ Insect repellent	☐ Salt tablets
☐ Wool sweater/shirt	☐ Hat
☐ Toilet tissue and trowel	☐ Ditty bag
☐ Watch	☐ Sunscreen

Adirondack Park Fire Towers with a Bright Future

Mount Arab

8-13-09

Round-trip Distance: 2.0 mi (3.2 km)
Elevation Change: 760 ft (232 m)
Summit Elevation: 2545 ft (776 m)
Difficulty: (1) Short, with varying grades.
Maps: Piercefield 7.5'

Mount Arab hosts one of the only two remaining fire towers in St. Lawrence County. (The other is Cathedral Rock in Wanakena.) A wooden tower was built on Mount Arab in 1912 and replaced in 1918 with the steel tower that currently adorns the summit. The tower and ground-level fire observer's cabin were last staffed in the 1980s. Subsequently, the tower, though popular for its views, deteriorated and in 1993 was condemned for public use.

In the spring of 1997, a citizen's group, the Friends of Mount Arab, was established with the early endorsement and support of the St. Lawrence County Planning Commission. The county legislature and several local governments later added their support. Adirondack Architectural Heritage (AARCH) agreed to handle the Friends' funds as a nonprofit extension of its mission in architectural preservation. The New York State DEC Region 6 was most helpful as well.

Restoration of the tower began on August 1, 1998. Major financial support has come from several ADK chapters, school groups, camp owners, local residents, and the DEC. By the summer of 1999, $12,000 in fundraising had allowed work that again made the tower safe for climbing. Further improvements are planned for the tower. The observer's cabin has been restored as a small museum and as a base for a summer interpreter. For more information, see Appendix A.

Although the top of the mountain is Forest Preserve land, the trail traverses land owned by John Hancock Insurance Company and International Paper Company. A conservation easement from Wagner Woodlands, which manages the John Hancock property, allows access to this attractive mountain, except during the autumn big-game rifle season, as noted on trailhead signage. The Mount Arab Trail, marked with red DEC disks, was rebuilt in July 1999 by Friends of Mount Arab with help from AmeriCorps volunteers.

▶ Trailhead: Access is off Conifer Road (County Route 62), which intersects NY 3 about 7.0 mi west of the intersection of NY 3 and NY 30 in Tupper Lake Village and 10.4 mi east of the intersection of

NY 3 and NY 56 in Seveys Corners. Follow Conifer Road 1.8 mi
south to the Eagle Crag Lake Road on the left. Follow this road 0.9
mi to the trailhead on the left, 0.3 mi after crossing the tracks of
the old railroad from Remsen to Lake Placid. The Town of
Piercefield's highway department constructed an enlarged parking
area in 1998 on the right side of the road opposite the trailhead. ◀

After a stand of medium-sized hardwoods at the outset, the trail
begins to rise immediately. The trail continues the steep climb until 0.8 mi, where it begins to level off amidst large outcrops of
granite. About 100 feet to the right at this point there is a fine overlook of the hamlet of Conifer, as well as Eagle Crag and Mount
Arab Lakes. The trail then begins to circle and finally reaches the
summit at 1.0 mi. Mountain ash and cherry on the summit indicate
fires in the early years of the century.

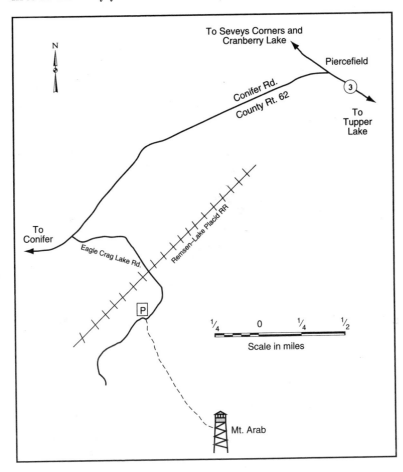

In the center of the small clearing at the top stands an observer's cabin and the restored fire tower. Mount Arab Lake and Eagle Crag Lake are nearby to the south-southeast, while Mount Matumbla, the highest in St. Lawrence County, is directly north. To the north-northeast, Raquette Pond and Tupper Lake Village can be clearly seen, while Mount Morris looms due east. Moosehead Mountain is visible to the north-northwest. The summits of these surrounding mountains are all on private land or blocked by private land and are therefore unavailable to the hiking public. All can be seen to be of approximately the same elevation as Mount Arab.

Trail in winter: Though ideal for a short, vigorous snowshoe climb, this trail is not recommended for skiing in winter due to steepness of terrain.

Azure Mountain

Round-trip Distance: 2.0 mi (3.2 km)
Elevation Change: Est. 700 ft (214 m)
Summit Elevation: 2518 ft (770 m)
Difficulty: (1) Short and pleasant, with switchbacks.
Maps: Lake Ozonia 7.5' and Meno 7.5'

This is a short, steep climb to one of the isolated northern Adirondack peaks. An Aermotor steel tower sits on the summit, restored in 2002 by the Azure Mountain Friends in cooperation with DEC.

▶ Trailhead: Access to this DEC red-marked trail is from the Blue Mountain Road, which heads south from NY 458 at a point approximately 4.0 mi south of St. Regis Falls and 3.0 mi north of the hamlet of Santa Clara. Proceed 7.0 mi south on Blue Mountain Road until a dirt road enters on the right. It is 0.1 mi down the dirt road to a gate. There is a parking lot on the left, about half way to the gate. (Note: One can also approach Azure Mountain from the south by an 18.3-mi drive from Paul Smiths along Keese Mills Road, which becomes the Blue Mountain Road north of Keese Mills.) ◀

The trail begins at the gate and passes a DEC register at about 100 yds. The trail is fairly level up to the site of a former fire observer's cabin at 0.3 mi. DEC has built a stone fireplace here. The trail begins to rise immediately afterwards, passing through a pole-sized maple grove with occasional white ash. At 0.5 mi both white and yellow birch begin to appear. This usually indicates a past burn.

The trail now starts to weave in and out of an eroded herd path that proceeds straight up the slope of the mountain. Avoid this route, created by placement of a former phone line to the summit fire tower. The switchback trail criss-crosses the old herd path for the rest of the steep pitch and eventually reaches the crest of the hill at 0.9 mi, with the mostly open summit slightly beyond at 1.0 mi.

The summit is crowned by the 1918 steel fire tower, now restored and safe for public use. In early October the summit is festooned

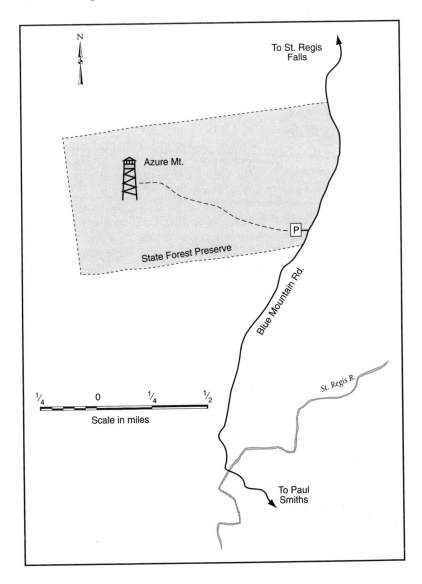

with pin cherry and chokecherry in fruit. It is laced with trails through the shrubbery made by bears in quest of fruit. Mount Marcy and the Seward Range can be seen to the south; the pointed summit of White-face Mountain to the southeast; and DeBar Mountain looms large to the east, while below lie some of the shimmering ponds of the St. Regis Canoe Area. From ground level, trees block the view north-ward, but restoration of the fire tower provides a view of farmlands and settlements of the St. Lawrence Valley.

Trail in winter: Cross-country skiers may find the upper trail too steep; snowshoers should have no trouble.

Bald (Rondaxe) Mountain

6-20-09

Round-trip Distance: 2.0 mi (3.2 km)
Elevation Change: 390 ft (119 m)
Summit Elevation: 2350 ft (716 m)
Difficulty: (1) Short hike, with only one minor
                         steep spot.
Maps: ADK West-Central Region map (C-3)
                         or Old Forge 7.5'

The short trail climbs through woods, and then through progressively more open rocky areas to the fire tower at the open summit of Bald Mountain, with great views. The steel fire tower, dating from 1917, is not staffed, but is climbable due to the restoration work of Friends of Bald Mt. and DEC in 2004–2005.

Looking from Bald Mountain over the Fulton Chain of lakes.

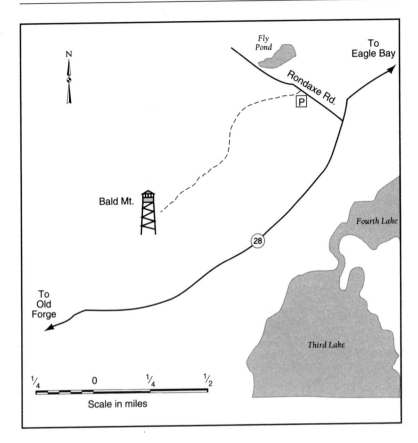

▶ Trailhead: From the Tourist Information Center in Old Forge, drive 4.5 mi northeast on NY 28, turn left (northwest) on Rondaxe Road, and after 0.2 mi, park in the large parking area on the left. From the village of Eagle Bay at the junction of NY 28 and Big Moose Road, drive 4.5 mi west and southwest on NY 28 and then turn right on Rondaxe Road. There are red trail markers and a DEC register box a few yards up the trail. ◀

The well-used trail ascends to the south, mostly along moderate grades, although there are some steep pitches. As one climbs, the deciduous forest soon gives way to an attractive spruce-fir forest. A large part of the ascent is on bedrock. Starting at 0.4 mi, fine views are to be had of Second, Third, and Fourth Lakes from the edge of cliffs on the left. The final 600 ft to the fire tower on the summit is mostly along the rock spine, with many viewing places. Trees near the summit and its approaches are mostly spruce and fir with white pine on the sunnier south-facing slopes. There is a scattering

Tillie Helms

Hikers ascend the tower on Bald (Rondaxe) Mountain. Author stands at left with trail description on his clipboard.

of mountain ash as well—its autumnal red leaves and berries form a stunning canopy against the backdrop of evergreens. The summit and tower are reached at 0.9 mi.

The open views from the summit embrace First through Fourth Lakes of the Fulton Chain to the south and east, part of Little Moose Lake to the south beyond First and Second Lakes, Blue

Mountain (3759 ft) in the distance to the east-northeast, and other mountains to the east. Climbing the fire tower makes the view more extensive, and on very clear days one may see several of the High Peaks, including Mount Marcy, the highest of the Adirondack peaks (5344 ft), 55 miles away, on the northeast horizon to the left of Blue Mountain.

Continuing southwest of the fire tower another 375 ft along the rock crest, one passes another fine vantage point or two and reaches a balanced rock of sorts, a boulder standing on a sloping ledge near the drop-off.

Trail in winter: Ascent on snowshoes is possible, but only experts should ski this trail. Crampons may be needed on the icy summit. Extra care is needed on the open rock slopes.

Belfry Mountain

Round-trip Distance:	0.6 mi (1.0 km)
Elevation Change:	120 ft (36.6 m)
Summit Elevation:	1820 ft (558 m)
Difficulty:	(1) Very short walk, moderately inclined.
Maps:	Witherbee 7.5'

The 1917 fire tower was partially restored and painted in 1999. A visit is a real treat—a short walk and a fantastic view, heaven for

casual strollers and small children. High Peaks Audubon members come up here to watch hawks fly low over the peak during their fall and spring migrations. It is possible to see a few hawks soaring at other times, too, so bring your binoculars. The location is above the abandoned mining area in the town of Moriah, Essex County, and northwest of Port Henry on Lake Champlain.

▶ Trailhead: From Exit 30 of I-87, ꞏꞏn south on NY 9 for 0.1 mi and ꞏꞏ left on Essex County Rt. 6 ꞏy Road; note sign to Witherbee,

This tower doubles as a communications relay station.

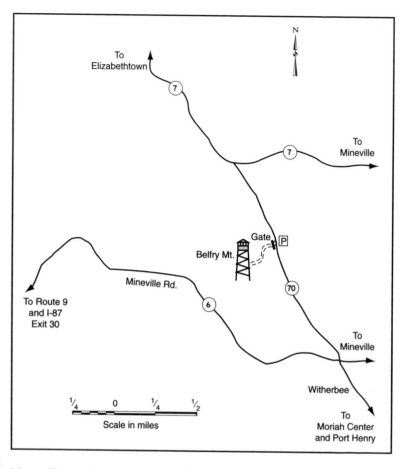

Mineville, and Port Henry). Proceed eastward for 7.6 mi to a four-way stop at County Rt. 70 in Witherbee. Turn left (north) on Rt. 70, driving 1.0 mi to a height of land with ample roadside parking on the right and a yellow steel gate on the left.

From Exit 31 of I-87, turn west on NY 9N. At 3.8 mi, just before reaching Elizabethtown, where NY 9N turns sharply right, turn left on Essex County Rt. 7. Continue south along Rt. 7, crossing over I-87 at 7.4 mi, and the causeway across Lincoln Pond at 9.6 mi. At 12.4 mi, bear right on County Rt. 70, driving 0.3 mi to a height of land with a yellow-gated road on the right. Park just off Rt. 70 opposite the gate on the left side. (Note: County Rt.7 can be reached from Elizabethtown directly by taking NY 9N 0.4 mi eastward from its northern junction with NY 9.)

From Port Henry, follow County Rt. 4 west to Moriah Center, then turn north on County Rt. 70 through Witherbee to the four-way stop sign mentioned in the first set of directions, above. Straight ahead 1.0 mi along Rt. 70 brings you to the trailhead on the left, with parking on the right. ◄

The route follows the gravel access road behind the gate for 0.2 mi to a radio tower and utility building on the right. The summit and fire tower are reached at 0.3 mi.

From the fire tower there are good views of Lake Champlain to the southeast with the Green Mountains of Vermont across most of the eastern horizon. Mineville and the slag heaps left over from the days of the iron mines can be seen below. The fire tower atop Hurricane Mountain is visible with binoculars to the northwest. Behind Hurricane and to its left is Whiteface Mountain. Further left and much closer to Belfry are Rocky Ridge and Giant Mountains, and to their left to the southwest, much of the Great Range and the Dixes. In the distance to the south-southwest is Pharoah Mountain.

Trail in winter: This short, gravel road makes a good ascent on either skis or snowshoes.

Black Mountain

The Black Mountain fire tower dates from 1918, but is now closed to the public. The fire tower and much of the small, rocky summit have been taken over by public service radio antennas. A windmill was built around 1996 to power one of the radio installations, but it appears to have been a faulty installation. The structure made a furious sound in high winds and rattled itself to death within a year. The windmill has been repaired and still makes a loud fluttering sound.

Despite these detractions from the hiker's enjoyment of the summit, there are striking views of Lake George and its surroundings. A climb of this prominent point is highly recommended. Black Mountain, located on the east side of Lake George, is the highest mountain in the Lake George area.

Black Mountain from the East

Round-trip Distance:	5.0 mi (8.1 km)
Elevation Change:	1046 ft (319 m)
Summit Elevation:	2646 ft (807 m)
Difficulty:	(2) Reasonably level for first mile, then very steep toward the top.
Maps:	ADK Eastern Region map (F-7) or Shelving Rock 7.5'

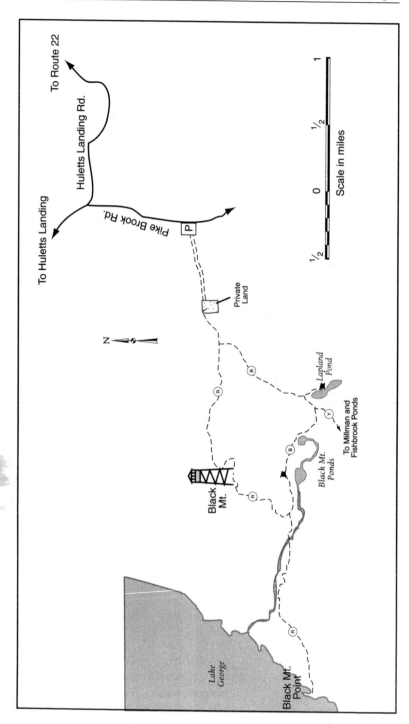

Because this trail, from Pike Brook Road, starts at 1600 ft elevation, it is a climb of only 1046 ft to the summit at 2646 ft. By contrast, the ascent from the shoreline of Lake George on the west trail from Black Mountain Point is 2300 ft. (See description following this one.)

▶ Trailhead: From a point on NY 22 about 7 mi north of Whitehall and 17 mi south of Ticonderoga, turn west on Huletts Landing Road (County Rt. 6) and drive 2.7 mi, then turn left onto Pike Brook Rd. At 0.8 mi on Pike Brook Road, the trailhead parking lot and register for Black Mountain are on the right. ◀

From the parking lot, the route follows an old road that bears red trail markers; avoid another old road to the right at 0.2 mi. At 0.5 mi the road reaches an old farmhouse and barn. It turns right here and passes behind the farm.

At 1.0 mi the trail reaches a junction. The trail to the left goes to Lapland, Millman, and Fishbrook Ponds; Black Mountain is straight ahead. The road has been gently uphill and almost level to this point.

At 1.3 mi the road divides; take the left fork. At 1.4 mi the trail crosses a wet place. It soon crosses a lovely brook tumbling across shelving rocks and at 1.6 mi crosses the brook at another junction, where a snowmobile trail enters and then veers off again. The trail goes left along the stream. It becomes steep, going up a small rock staircase. At 1.7 mi it ascends bare rock next to the stream. Now the trail is washed out. At 2.0 mi it follows a small streambed, then it cuts right, away from the stream.

At 2.1 mi the trail becomes very steep in a fern-filled glen. At 2.2 mi avoid the snowmobile trail that branches off to the right. The trail divides again. These forks rejoin; the left fork enters a clearing with a huge open rock. Ahead are the observer's cabin, toolshed, and woodshed. At 2.5 mi the trail reaches the closed tower and the elaborate radio installation. There is a view the length of Lake George, except for the Narrows, which is obstructed by the west shoulder of the mountain. For a view of the Narrows and the rest of Lake George to the southwest, follow the trail a short distance down to the west. A herd path to the right leads to open rock ledges.

Sugarloaf Mountain, directly to the northeast, has a transmitter tower on top. Elephant Mountain to the north obstructs a view of Huletts Landing. Bluff Point is the first point in view on the east shore, with Sabbath Day Point across on the west shore.

Trail in winter: This is a nice snowshoe trail with some fairly steep climbing near the top. Instep crampons may be useful for icy sections.

Black Mountain from Black Mountain Point

Round-trip Distance: 5.6 mi (9.0 km)
Elevation Change: 2300 ft (701 m)
Summit Elevation: 2646 ft (807 m)
Difficulty: (3) Steep and unrelenting climb.
Maps: ADK Eastern Region map (E-7)
                                or Shelving Rock 7.5'

The top of Black Mountain provides some of the finest views in the Lake George region; this trail from the shoreline of Lake George is the most spectacular way to climb to the top. It is the lesser used of the two trails up Black Mountain, but definitely the more interesting of the two. Leaving the shoreline at one of the wildest remaining areas of the lake, and then climbing past waterfalls and over open rock ledges on the way to the summit, the trail gives the hiker a feel of what it may have been like when this region was a summer home for Native Americans hundreds of years ago.

▶ Trailhead: The trail begins at the north end of the Lakeside Trail at Black Mountain Point, which is accessible by boat, or by one of the many trails from the Shelving Rock area to the south. The trail is also accessible from the summit of Black Mountain via the trail from Pike Brook Road (see preceding description), which is marked with red markers. ◀

From the junction with the Lakeside Trail at Black Mountain Point, the trail to Black Mountain heads steeply uphill to the east. At 0.3 mi, it crosses an expanse of bedrock, then soon moderates as it meanders through a forest of tall hemlocks. The trail soon crosses a brook and climbs again until at 0.6 mi it levels off briefly and bends to the left. At 0.7 mi climbing begins again, past a small gorge on the left. The trail bends right, away from the gorge and to the east. A short detour off the trail will bring you to a number of pretty cascades and flumes just out of sight of the trail.

At 0.8 mi the route makes a switchback to the left, not far from more rushing water. Soon the trail parallels another gorge along the stream on the left, and at 1.1 mi the cascades in the stream are once again visible from the trail.

The trail soon bends right, away from the stream, heading up over bare rock. At 1.3 mi the trail climbs steeply along a huge rock filled with moss, lichens, and ferns on the left. It soon crosses a stream, then briefly levels off. At 1.6 mi a wooden bridge crosses a stream, just below a small waterfall. The junction with the Black Mountain Ponds Trail is reached at 1.8 mi. To the right are Black Mountain Pond and Lapland Pond; to the left, the summit of Black Mountain.

Heading left, the trail climbs to 2.0 mi where it passes a huge rock wall on the right and then comes to a rocky outcrop with a nice view. Just off the trail there's a rock ledge that overlooks Black Mountain Pond and Round Pond. The trail levels off briefly, then climbs up several switchbacks with some nice views, reaching a side trail on the right at 2.6 mi. This trail leads to a grassy clearing and ledges with a great view of Lake George and many of the islands to the south. Below are Black Mountain Pond, Round Pond, and Lapland Pond farther east.

The main trail soon passes a slanting rock wall, then heads over bare rock with more views to the left. It reaches the closed fire tower at the summit at 2.8 mi, where it meets the trail from Pike Brook Road.

Trail in winter: This route is a great snowshoe trip after a good snowfall, but access is difficult. Black Mountain Point can be reached only across Lake George, or from Shelving Rock Mountain trailhead.

Blue Mountain   10-10-09

Round-trip Distance: 4.0 mi (6.4 km)
Elevation Change: 1550 ft (473 m)
Summit Elevation: 3759 ft (1146 m)
Difficulty: (2) Some steep areas in middle section.
Maps: ADK Central Region map (M-9)
or Blue Mountain Lake 7.5'

The fire tower on Blue Mountain was selected by the Adirondack Mountain Club (ADK) in 1993 to draw attention to fire towers' restoration potential throughout the Forest Preserve. The Blue Mountain tower was chosen because of its popularity (15,000 visitors a year), its historic value (built in 1917), its trailhead location on a major paved highway, and its proximity to the Adirondack Museum. Leadership in this model restoration was later assumed by the Cornell Cooperative Extension agent for Hamilton County, along with the DEC forest ranger and Indian Lake's town supervisor. In summer 1994, the tower was revitalized, and an interpreter intern hired, with funds supplied by Hamilton County, to greet the public at the summit. The trail to the summit is a self-guided nature walk with interpretive pamphlets (available at the trailhead) keyed to numbered posts along the trail.

First named To-war-loon-da, the Hill of Storms, by the Iroquois, the mountain was renamed Mount Clinch, after a state assembly-man who supported the Eckford survey of 1811. (The lake was named Lake Janet, after Eckford's daughter.) Fortunately, the many thousands of annual visitors to this area don't have to climb Mount Clinch from Lake Janet. Blue Mountain is now the name of the summit from which Verplanck Colvin's Adirondack Survey crews set off their bright explosions each night, which permitted them to synchronize their chronometers, improving the accuracy of their determinations of latitude and longitude based on observations of the sun.

Perhaps because it is so accessible from a major highway, Blue Mountain has been one of the most frequently climbed Adirondack peaks for over a century.

▶ Trailhead: The trailhead is on the east side of NY 30/28N at a height of land 1.4 mi north of the intersection of Rts. 30, 28, and 28N in the hamlet of Blue Mountain Lake and 0.1 mi up the hill from the Adirondack Museum. This height of land is about 9.5 mi south of the junction of Routes 30 and 28N in Long Lake. There is ample parking on private property at the trailhead. ◀

The trail heads east from the parking area, following red trail markers. (Avoid the red-marked DEC trail that heads north to Tirrell Pond.) A barrier cable blocks vehicular use. The flat logging road swings southeast and then gradually gains elevation. At 0.2 mi, the trail enters woods, soon crossing a creek. Elevation continues to be gained at a comfortable rate.

At 0.9 mi, a moderate grade begins, but soon eases. Then the route steepens until it climbs over bare rock sheets. The grade finally levels at 1.5 mi and heads northeast through attractive spruce.

The last 0.5 mi is very enjoyable. The trail ends at the summit at 2.0 mi. Some views are gained from the flat-topped summit at ground level, but excellent views require climbing the fire observer's tower. To the west is Blue Mountain Lake. To its left is Eagle Lake and beyond it Utowana Lake. Raquette Lake is visible beyond the ridges. To the north are Minnow Pond, Mud Pond, South Pond, and finally part of Long Lake. To the northeast is Tirrell Mountain with beautiful Tirrell Pond below. Just to the left is Tongue Mountain. Algonquin Mountain is seen in line with Tongue Mountain 25 mi to the northeast in the High Peaks. To the right of the gap by Algonquin are Avalanche Pass and then Mount Colden. Somewhat farther left of Algonquin are Ampersand Mountain and the Seward Range. Much closer is Kempshall Mountain on the east shore of Long Lake.

Trail in winter: Blue Mountain is an excellent snowshoe climb.

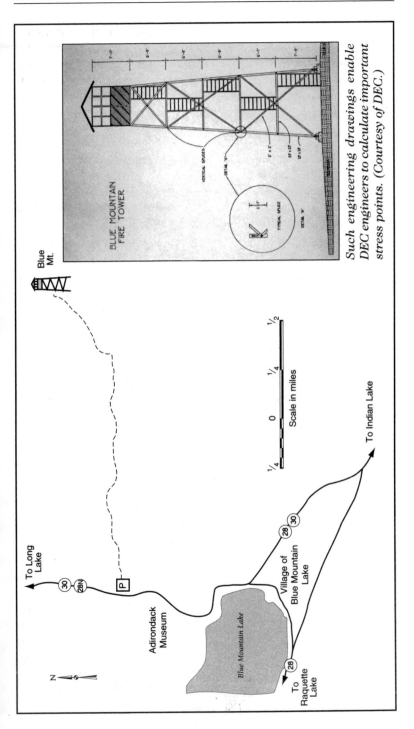

Such engineering drawings enable DEC engineers to calculate important stress points. (Courtesy of DEC.)

Cathedral Rock

Round-trip Distance: 2.4 mi (3.8 km) 8 - 13 - 09
Elevation Change: 185 ft (56 m) 10 - 12 - 09
Summit Elevation: 1725 ft (526 m)
Difficulty: (1) Pleasant walk, mostly along forest roads, with a steep pitch near the end.
Maps: Newton Falls 7.5'

This fire tower is on land of the Ranger School of the State University of New York College of Environmental Science and Forestry at Wanakena. The materials were salvaged in 1971, with DEC permission, by the school's students and faculty from an abandoned tower that once stood atop Tooley Pond Mountain, five miles northwest of Cranberry Lake. Reconstruction of the tower on Cathedral Rock began in the 1980s; the cab was essentially finished by volunteer and alumni labor in summer 1999. Windows and final restoration measures were completed in 2000. The school allows access by the public, requesting that hikers park in one of the parking lots described below. Cathedral Rock and Mount Arab sport the only two fire towers left in St. Lawrence County, both built by the Aermotor Company of Chicago in 1918.

For additional information on the tower's restoration and maintenance, see Appendix A.

▶ Trailhead: From NY Rt. 3 between the villages of Star Lake and Cranberry Lake, turn south on County Rt. 61, the short side road shown on most highway maps as leading toward the village of Wanakena. After 0.8 mi, bear left at the first

The rotating "stan-helio" signal atop this tower reflects the sun's rays in all directions. This "tin sun" is a replica of the signal used by Verplanck Colvin to locate particular summits from great distances.

junction. Turn left again in 0.2 mi on Ranger School Road, bypassing Wanakena's central hamlet area. Proceed another 1.2 mi along this road to a left turn into the campus at the first sign marking one's arrival at the Ranger School. At a T-junction 0.1 mi further, turn left. Drive another 0.1 mi into a large parking lot with a gated

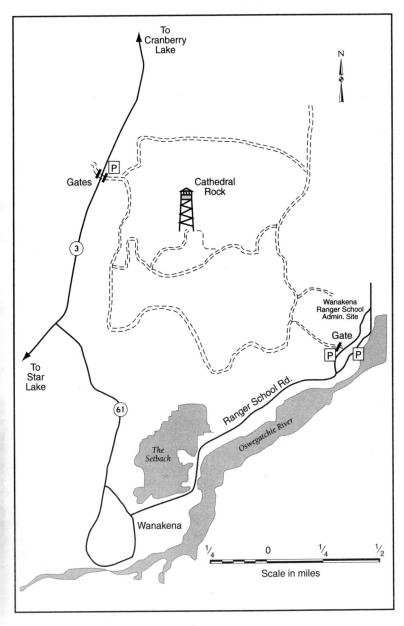

gravel road on the right. Park in the lot and begin your hike at the gate. Public parking is also available off Ranger School Road in front of the school, down along the river, and should be used on weekdays when the school is in session. ◀

From the gate, walk down the gravel road, passing a white utility building on your right. At 0.2 mi, keep right where a road enters from the left. At 0.3 mi, a road branches right into an open area leveled by the microburst storm of July 1995, but the hiker continues straight ahead. Turn on a road to the left at 0.6 mi. At 0.9 mi, a red-marked foot trail bears off the road to the right through a white pine plantation. About 70 yds further, where a side trail goes right, keep straight ahead beginning a steeper climb up Cathedral Rock. The trail switchbacks right, then left along rocky ledges to a student lean-to at 1.2 mi. Turn right at the lean-to and follow the trail west-northwest 90 yds to the fire tower at the top of the hill at 1.2 mi.

ADKer Carol Mantell pauses near Cathedral Rock tower, with surveyor's wheel used to measure the trail

The tower provides otherwise unobtainable views of nearby Cranberry Lake and the glacial hills in this region of the Adirondack Park. Algonquin Peak in the High Peaks, 48 mi to the east, can be discerned on a very clear day, especially when it is snow-covered, poking its head above the nearer Seward Range.

Note: The tower can also be reached from a gated road leading directly off NY 3 about 0.7 mi toward Cranberry Lake from the turnoff to Wanakena. Hiking distance from NY 3 is about 1.4 mi. See page map.

Trail in winter: Most of the gravel roads shown on the page map are not plowed, but make good ski or snowshoe routes. The red-marked foot trail at 0.9 mi is too steep for skis. Skiers should use the road to the summit, about one-quarter mile farther west.

Goodnow Mountain

Round-trip Distance: 3.8 mi (6.1 km)
Elevation Change: 1040 ft (317 m)
Summit Elevation: 2690 ft (820 m)
Difficulty: (2) A moderate climb over a moderate
                         distance.
Maps: Newcomb 7.5'   .

Not only does this peak offer a marvelous view of the High Peaks from its restored 1922 fire tower, but the trail to the summit is now a self-guided nature walk with interpretive pamphlets (available at the trailhead) that are keyed to marked posts along the trail. This hike is now a perfect complement to the displays at the Visitor Interpretive Center at Newcomb. A new parking area and 0.9 mi of new trail were completed in the summer of 1993. The new route adds 0.4 mi to the overall distance to the summit.

The trail is entirely on the private land of the Archer and Anna Huntington Forest, owned by the College of Environmental Science and Forestry (ESF) in Syracuse. It is ESF students and faculty at the Adirondack Ecological Center who produced the interpretive pamphlets and coordinated a grant that enabled the Town of Newcomb to hire a work crew. The latter built the new parking area and trail—a trail complete with frequent benches for resting. ESF staff continue to maintain the fire tower. Because this is private land, no camping or fires are permitted, and the area is closed from sunset to sunrise. No hunting is permitted on this private preserve, so this is a good choice for hikers who are concerned about possible danger during the hunting season.

▶ Trailhead: The trail starts on the south side of Rt. 28N, 1.5 mi west of the entrance to the Visitor Interpretive Center west of the hamlet of Newcomb. This point is 11.4 mi east of Long Lake. A large white sign marks the turn to a new parking area and a kiosk that contains a register and interpretive pamphlets. ◀

The trail is marked by red markers with small black arrows. From the parking area, the trail climbs moderately for 200 yds before swinging right and continuing, with small rises and falls, along a shelf parallel to the highway. Reaching a bridge across a small brook at 0.5 mi, the trail swings left and at 0.7 mi begins to climb moderately. After a steady climb, the trail reaches the crest of a ridge at 0.9 mi, where it joins the old trail.

Swinging sharply left, the trail descends slightly before climbing gradually to 1.1 mi. The route steepens there, then levels just

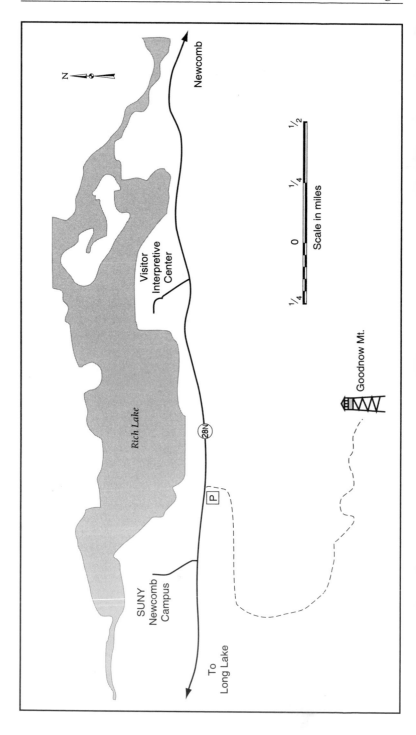

In the cab atop the Goodnow tower, former Cornell Cooperative Extension agent Jim Briggs studies the sighting map that was once used to spot fires

before passing a concrete platform on the right at 1.4 mi. A side trail, right, in a notch at 1.5 mi leads to a covered well and small horse barn. The trail becomes a rocky path and steepens again. Spruce and balsam fir close in. Open rock at 1.8 mi provides a view to the right. Then, after dropping into a small depression, a long gradual incline leads to the rocky summit and fire tower at 1.9 mi. There are some views to the east and south from ground level, but from the tower one can see 23 of the major peaks. The Santanoni Range is close by to the northwest, Algonquin Peak and Mount Marcy are particularly prominent to the north, and Vanderwhacker Mountain with its tower is seen to the east.

Trail in winter: The new start for this trail is narrower and steeper than the original route. It is no longer feasible as a ski trip, but its short distance and the absence of any really steep terrain make it an ideal introductory snowshoe trip. Measure driving mileage carefully. High drifts sometimes make trailhead location difficult.

Gore Mountain

Round-trip Distance:	9.0 mi (14.4 km)
Elevation Change:	2533 ft (772 m)
Summit Elevation:	3583 ft (1092 m)
Difficulty:	(4) A long hike; significant elevation gain with intermittent steep sections.
Maps:	ADK Central Region map (B-6) or Thirteenth Lake 7.5'

The Gore Mountain fire tower dates from 1918, and though it is not in too sad condition, it suffers from proximity to the Gore ski facilities and is encrusted with myriad radio and microwave relay antennas. Its value as a lookout and educational site for skiers in winter and for the general public in snowless months has apparently not yet been discovered by the Olympic Regional Development Authority, which manages the state-run ski area.

The trail to the summit of Gore is named in honor of the Schaefer brothers, Carl, Paul, and Vincent. Paul was a renowned Adirondack conservationist and writer, while Carl and Vincent were major figures in developing skiing on the mountain before the present facility was constructed. The brainchild of Paul's son-in-law, Don Greene, the trail was designed, cut, and marked by Don and other volunteers. It is entirely on public land.

Caution is advised for 200 yds on each side of Dave's Cirque and for 50 yds beyond Paul's Ledge, since mountain bike trails overlap the Schaefer Trail in these locations.

▶ Trailhead: The trailhead is located at the North Creek Ski Bowl. Approaching from the south on NY 28, turn left onto Ski Bowl Road 0.3 mi north of the NY 28/28N intersection at North Creek. There is a large DEC sign for the trail at the turn, and the North Creek Health Center is on the left. There is another DEC sign for the Schaefer Trail 0.3 mi down Ski Bowl Road on the right. Park across from the sign. Maps are available in the trail register, which is on a knoll above the sign. ◀

From the DEC sign, follow blue DEC trail markers southwest up the right side of the ski slope. The ski slope levels briefly at 0.2 mi, then continues up steeply to 0.5 mi, where the ski slope turns right and the trail crosses left and enters the woods.

The trail turns right at an arrow sign at 0.6 mi. It climbs steeply and bears right on a ski trail at 0.7 mi. At 0.8 mi, it reenters the woods at a sign on the left side of the ski trail.

After crossing two streams, the trail continues up a moderate

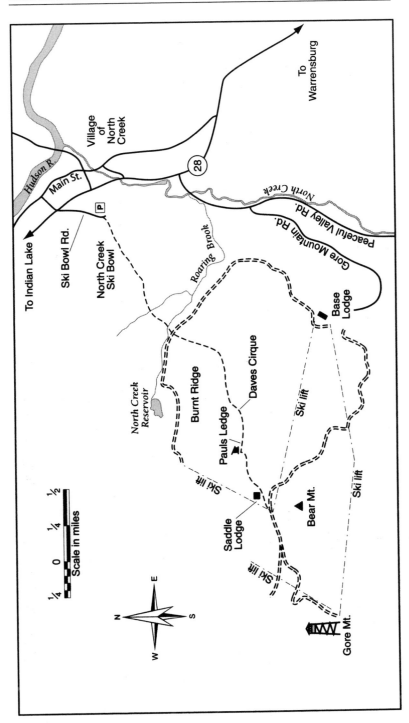

grade until dropping down to cross Roaring Brook at 1.2 mi just above a bridge. The trail immediately crosses a road and begins its climb up to the east shoulder of Burnt Ridge. It reaches a power line at 1.5 mi, with a view of NY 28 downhill to the left. The trail angles left through a raspberry patch to a right turn sign on the opposite side. It follows the power line briefly before turning left into the woods, heading generally south.

The trail climbs steeply, then continues on a level course until dropping down a moderate slope to a stream at 2.1 mi. The trail was purposely routed here for the hiker's enjoyment. The stream runs through Dave's Cirque, a beautiful open woods glade shaped like an amphitheater, with a rock wall defining its upper end.

Less than 100 yds from the stream, the trail passes a pile of rock slabs stacked domino-style against one another (Chanol's Rock) on the left. Passing another rock formation on the left, the trail bears right and climbs up a moderate slope. It parallels a rock wall on the right until turning left at 2.4 mi. The trail climbs up a short steep pitch to Paul's Ledge at 2.5 mi. Crane Mountain can be seen to the south, while Bear Mountain is directly ahead to the west. From here, the trail circles around to the right (north) toward Bear Mountain. Just past Paul's Ledge, 50 ft to the right of the main trail, there is a lean-to.

Leaving the ledge, the trail drops down into a sag, bypasses a swampy area to the left, and continues up a short steep pitch to a ski trail at 2.9 mi. The High Peaks, centered by Marcy, can be seen to the north from the middle of the slope.

Angling left up the slope, the trail continues into the woods. Immediately before another ski slope at 3.1 mi, the trail turns left. It emerges into the open in 150 yds, turns right up a ski trail and reaches Saddle Lodge at 3.3 mi.

From the lodge, the trail follows Cloud Trail to the top of the mountain. (A map of the ski trails is on the right just beyond Saddle Lodge.) It continues past ski lifts on a level course to 3.7 mi, where it turns left and climbs steeply to a right turn at 3.8 mi. From there, it follows the maintenance road as it climbs, often steeply, to the top of Cloud Trail. The trail ends at the fire tower to the right of Cloud Trail at 4.5 mi.

If the fire tower is closed, a variety of views can be found by wandering around the top of the mountain. Particularly notable is the view of the High Peaks from the crest of Cloud Trail.

Trail in winter: Winter use of the trail is permitted only as far as Paul's Ledge. The trail beyond is closed to climbers during skiing season. Though Paul's Ledge is a rewarding destination for a snowshoe climb, the author hopes that eventually a new trail will be opened for year-round access to the summit.

Hadley Mountain

5/24/09

Round-trip Distance:	3.6 mi (5.8 km)
Elevation Change:	1525 ft (465 m)
Summit Elevation:	2675 ft (815 m)
Difficulty:	(2) A short hike with a steady ascent and a level section in the middle.
Maps:	ADK Southern Region map (J-6) or Conklingville 7.5', Lake Luzerne 7.5', and Stony Creek 7.5'

Some of the most spectacular views in the southern Adirondacks are obtained by hiking to the bare summit of Hadley Mountain. The 1916 40-ft Aermotor fire tower there was restored in 1995 and 1996 by the Hadley Fire Tower Committee with help from the DEC ranger corps. Since 1996, from July 4th weekend until Labor Day, the Committee has employed an interpreter to staff the summit facilities, which include a ranger cabin and small storage shed. Significant grants from the International Paper Company Foundation have provided much of the funds for this summit guide position, while donations for the committee's restoration work have come from residents of all the neighboring communities, Adirondack Mountain Club chapters, local community organizations, and area businesses. For more information about this tower's restoration, maintenance, and summer staffing, see Appendix A.

The entire West Mountain Ridge, of which Hadley Mountain is the highest point, and much of the surrounding forests were burned over in 1903, 1908, 1911, and again in 1915. A rusted iron sign, erected in 1936, reminded the visitor of this sad history. The sign was vandalized and stolen in 1991, another sad story. A new historical marker (2000) contains unfortunate factual errors.

The trail to the summit serves as a self-guided nature walk. Interpretive pamphlets, available at the trailhead, are keyed to numbers posted along the trail.

▶ Trailhead: Take NY 9N southwest from I-87 Exit 21 (or north from Corinth) to the village of Lake Luzerne. Turn west toward the Hudson River at the only traffic light along 9N, proceeding northwest 0.4 mi with the Hudson River on your left, into the business district. Turn left and cross the river into Hadley and continue 0.4

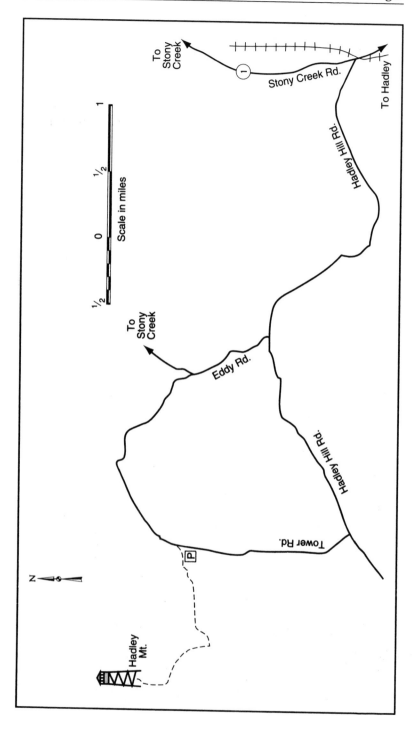

mi to a turn right (north) on Stony Creek Road (Saratoga County Rt. 1). After about 3 mi, just after crossing the railroad track, bear left (west) uphill on Hadley Hill Road. Proceed 4.5 mi to unpaved Tower Road on the right, which is marked with a road sign. Turn north (right) on Tower Road and drive for another 1.5 mi to the enlarged (1996) trailhead parking lot on the left. (Tower Road is usually in good driving condition for passenger cars, although in early spring there may be muddy areas and rocky washouts, especially along the sides of the road.) ◀

The trail begins at the far end of the parking area (sign the trail register here) and immediately leads at a moderate grade through mature hemlocks. The trail is marked with red DEC disks and is easy to follow due to severe erosion along the abandoned jeep trail as well as a good deal of use by hikers. Several sections have been worn down to bedrock, including an attractive area at 0.3 mi that resembles a slanted city sidewalk. In other areas, large rocks and boulders have been revealed to create an obstacle course.

Climbing continues through predominantly hardwood forest. The general direction is west, and the trail climbs steadily upward at a moderate pitch. There is a brief flat section where a small seasonal stream is crossed at 0.5 mi. Here an attractive large boulder makes a good resting place.

After crossing the stream, the trail bends right and continues to

Hadley Mountain tower after restoration in 1996. In addition to installing new windows, guy wires, and bolts, workers replaced all stairs and landings with pressure-treated lumber.

Richard Dean

Aerial view of the Hadley Mountain tower, observer's cabin, and tool shed, 1997

climb. At 0.6 mi, large glacial "erratics," or boulders, are seen on both sides of the trail. In winter, a cliff face on the right is noticeable for its colorful blue-green ice formations. The bedrock and these boulders are gneiss, a metamorphosed shale composed of silts washed down from Canada some 1.8 billion years ago.

Finally, a much steeper section of the trail culminates at the top of a ridge at 1.0 mi, a spot known as Panther Pass by local residents. A turn right begins a gentle section across the top of this rib of West Mountain Ridge. This is a most welcome part of the hike after the moderately steep but relentless climb.

At 1.2 mi after a brief upward grade, the trail swings left and passes through a grove of stunted oak, mountain ash, maple, and birch. Now headed in a northwest direction, the trail jogs right and begins a moderate climb.

At 1.3 mi, the marked trail swings to the left while a faint path continues straight ahead along the route of an old telephone line. Both routes lead to the summit, but the best trail for pre-summit views, and thus the most popular, is to the left.

Taking this left fork, climbing continues at a moderate rate of ascent until at 1.4 mi the trail reaches the first of a series of lookouts featuring views of the Great Sacandaga Reservoir. For the remaining 0.3 mi the trail slabs to the left (southwest) side of the ridgeline, traversing several open areas that grant the hiker marvelous vistas. At 1.7 mi, after the last rocky outlook, the trail levels briefly, then splits again, with the right fork leading 200 ft to the observer's cabin and the left making a slight climb to the summit and tower at 1.8 mi.

Here, on a clear day, the hiker enjoys a brilliant panorama, an ample reward for the effort expended. In addition to Great Sacandaga Reservoir to the south and nearby Spruce Mountain to the northwest, one can see Crane, Blue, Moose, Snowy, Baldhead, and Pharaoh Mountains. On a very clear day several of the High Peaks are visible on the northern skyline, the Green Mountains of Vermont in the northeast, and southward, the Helderberg and Catskill Mountains. A second Spruce Mountain, this one hosting a fire tower, can be seen to the south-southwest. It, too, is described in this guide.

An adventurous group with a map and compass can continue this hike by bushwhacking northward. The route begins as a faint herd path from the summit of Hadley across the north summit of West Mountain and on to the summit of Roundtop Mountain, which can be sighted from Hadley's tower. It's a small mountain with a bare summit and a pristine quality of peaceful isolation and unspoiled natural beauty. Be aware that in bushwhacking to Roundtop, hikers traverse private, though unposted, land.

Trail in winter: A great snowshoe hike. Distances are not as daunting as those required to climb many other mountains, and the climbing does not require special equipment (like crampons) under *normal* mid-winter conditions.

Kane Mountain

The short hike to the summit of Kane Mountain in northern Fulton County leads to a well-restored fire tower. Views are available only upon climbing the tower. There is also an observer's cabin and grassy picnic area on the summit. Trails lead down the east side as well as across the ridge and down the north slope, then east back to Green Lake or west to Pine Lake Campground. Pine Lake Campground, however, is privately owned and the owners discourage visiting hikers. In fact, they charge a $5 toll to cross through it in summer.

This summit is very popular with the summer residents of the nearby lakes area, and its fire tower was staffed until 1990. Abandoned by DEC, the tower deteriorated rapidly, but has been brought back to safe public use through efforts of the Canada Lake Protective Association and DEC. Beginning in 1995, volunteers and DEC replaced the floor of the cab, installed a railing around the trap door, and rehabilitated the nice observer's cabin. They have kept the summit site clean of trash. For more information on their ongoing efforts, or to make a contribution to the tower's continued maintenance, see Appendix A.

Kane Mountain via the East Trail

Round-trip Distance: 1.8 mi (2.9 km)
Elevation Change: 620 ft (189 m)
Summit Elevation: 2180 ft (664 m)
Difficulty: (2) A short hike of moderate grade.
Maps: ADK Southern Region map (C-10)
                         or Canada Lake 7.5' and Caroga Lake 7.5'

This is one of three trails up Kane Mountain.

▷ Trailhead: The east trail can be reached by turning northeast off NY 10/29A onto Green Lake Road just north of Green Lake. This turn is 3 mi north of the junction of NY 10 and NY 29A in the village of Caroga Lake and about 2 mi south of their northerly junction in Pine Lake. Drive 0.6 mi to the end of Green Lake, where there is a fork to the left. The road around the lake continues sharply to the right. Take the left fork, which is a less used dirt road. Within 200 yds there is a parking area on the right, with the marked trail to Kane Mountain on the left. The brown and yellow DEC sign says "Kane Mt. Observatory 0.5 mi," although the actual distance is 0.9 mi. ◁

The trail immediately begins to climb through a broad avenue of mature hardwoods. At 0.1 mi it bends right and at 0.2 mi continues through a series of small jogs left and right until at 0.6 mi it straightens out. The trail is moderately steep and well used, although trail markers seem to be less frequent as the ascent continues. There are a number of twists and turns in this old jeep road. As the

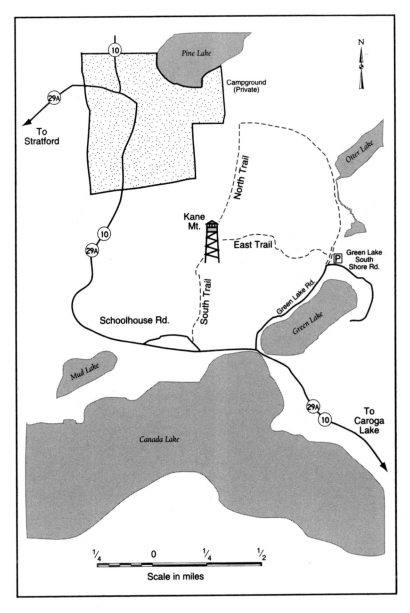

summit is approached the trail becomes level and passes through a
cleared area where numerous berry bushes appear to be trying to
gain a permanent foothold. The last several feet are through a grassy
clearing, then past the observer's cabin. The trail turns right to the
fire tower area, which is reached at 0.9 mi.

A loop trek is possible by returning across the summit ridge and
down the old north trail, then walking eastward on the abandoned
road at the foot of the mountain back to the trailhead. (See below.)

Trail in winter: An easy snowshoe trip, recommended for practice
in preparation for longer, more difficult treks.

Kane Mountain via the South and North Trails

Round-trip Distance: 1.4 mi (2.2 km)
Elevation Change: 580 ft (177 m)
Summit Elevation: 2180 ft (664 m)
Difficulty: (2) A short hike of moderate grade.
Maps: ADK Southern Region map (C-10)
                         or Canada Lake 7.5' and Caroga Lake 7.5'

▶ Trailhead: To reach the trailhead on the south side of the mountain, turn onto Schoolhouse Road from NY 10/29A. The road is
located on the north (right if driving west) side, approximately 0.4
mi west of Green Lake Road, which is also on the right. (See trailhead
description, above.) About 150 yds up this dirt road is the start of
the marked trail on the right. A parking area carved into the shoulder of the road is large enough for two or three cars. ◀

The trail immediately begins to climb at a moderately steep grade.
At 0.2 mi it is rocky and well used, but wide and clear. The forest is
open and is composed of a preponderance of sugar maples as well
as other hardwoods such as ash, yellow birch, and beech.

At 0.3 mi the climb becomes steeper, with sections of loose earth
and stone underfoot. A large tree trunk is lying at the side of the
trail, and a maple tree is growing in the center at 0.4 mi. At 0.5 mi
a few hemlocks come into view—their sporadic dark green against
the background of red and yellow maples makes a pretty scene in
the fall.

At 0.6 mi the fire tower comes into view. As the hiker approaches
the tower, the trail levels and the observer's cabin appears on the
right about 150 yds off the trail. The tower and cabin have been
restored and the tower can be climbed for excellent views. On a
good day, one can see south as far as the Catskills and north to the

High Peaks, while in the near distance Pine Lake to the northwest and West Canada Lake to the south are a delight to the eye.

Hikers wishing to make a circle trip and return to their cars via Green Lake and NY 10 may take the trail to the right which begins just past the cabin and heads due east through a clearing. The total round-trip distance is 1.5 mi.

A longer trek can also be had by traversing the summit ridge and descending on the North Trail, then turning right at the foot of the mountain and walking the old road circling around the base and returning to Green Lake. Although sporadically marked with yellow paint, this route is not as clear and easy as the other two. There's also quite a bit of blowdown in some areas, yet a descent of the mountain using this route takes one through scenic forest glens to reach the junction of the old road at 0.9 mi. Turn right (east) and hike another 0.8 mi past Fish Hatchery Pond to exit on Green Lake South Shore Road.

Trail in winter: A short snowshoe trek to the summit, which can be combined with a ski trek around the base of the mountain. Skiers can turn left at the foot of the mountain and traverse the Pine Lake Campground in winter.

Owls Head Mountain

Round-trip Distance:	6.2 mi (9.9 km)
Elevation Change:	1150 ft (350 m)
Summit Elevation:	2780 ft (847 m)
Difficulty:	(2) A moderate climb, steep at the end.
Maps:	Deerland 7.5'

The red-marked trail to the top of Owls Head Mountain starts at the outskirts of Long Lake village and ascends an isolated peak providing a panoramic view of the surrounding area. The 35-ft Aermotor steel fire tower dates from 1919, and was abandoned by the state in 1970. It was restored to safe public use in summer 2004 by DEC forest ranger Jim Waters, other DEC personnel, and the Friends of Owls Head Fire Tower.

A canoeing approach is available from the Lake Eaton campground off NY 30.

▶ Trailhead: Follow NY 30 north from the center of Long Lake to Endion Road on the left at the edge of the village. It is 1.6 mi on Endion Road to the trailhead parking lot on the right. Paddlers may canoe across Lake Eaton to a short, poorly marked

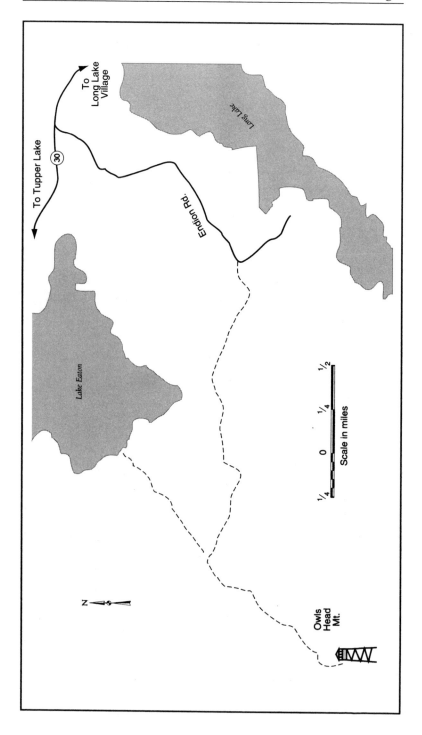

trail connecting to the Owls Head Mountain Trail. (See page map and description.) ◀

There are two more or less parallel trails at the outset. The trail to the right is marked as a snowmobile trail. The trail on the left immediately begins a steep climb under large hemlock and yellow birch. At 0.5 mi it levels off as sugar maples become prominent. The snowmobile trail comes in on the right, and the two trails run concurrently. At 0.8 mi, the snowmobile trail makes a slight detour to the right before rejoining the hiking trail after a short distance.

At 1.1 mi the trail reaches a junction with DEC signs. The trail right is the abandoned Lake Eaton Campground–Forked Lake Campground Trail to Lake Eaton. (Paddlers who cross Lake Eaton turn right to join the Owls Head Mountain Trail here.) The Owls Head Mountain Trail proceeds straight; it is now marked with both red hiking trail markers and the larger red snowmobile trail markers, since the abandoned Lake Eaton Campground–Forked Lake Campground Trail and the Owls Head Mountain Trail coincide for the next 0.3 mi. To add somewhat to the confusion, an occasional yellow snowmobile trail marker is encountered. The yellow markers were used by the DEC as snowmobile markers, but have recently been replaced by red markers on most trails. The signs at this and subsequent junctions are clear, however, so the variations in trail marker colors should not prove troublesome.

At 1.2 mi a recessed sign on the right marks the junction with the Lake Eaton Trail, a short, sporadically marked trail that leads to the shore of Lake Eaton. The Owls Head Mountain Trail continues under a canopy of hemlocks with occasional telephone poles still standing as testimony to the staffed fire tower that once stood on top of Owls Head.

At 1.4 mi the trail reaches another marked DEC junction. The abandoned Lake Eaton Campground–Forked Lake Campground Trail heads left for 8.2 mi to Forked Lake, while the Owls Head Mountain Trail again continues straight. Small red trail markers point the way; the red and yellow snowmobile disks indicate the trail to Forked Lake.

At 1.8 mi a steep ravine is passed on the left. Spruce now begins to come into the canopy. At 2.0 mi the trail begins to climb, getting rockier and steeper at 2.5 mi. Another ravine is passed on the left and large beech are now present. At 2.7 mi the way is encumbered slightly by blowdown until at 2.8 mi the remnants of the fire observer's cabin are passed in an open glade underneath the pinnacle of Owls Head.

The trail now begins a very steep scramble to the top, starting to rise just past the open glade. This last ascent is somewhat strenuous and may entail use of the hands in climbing. Finally at 3.1 mi the trail reaches the summit with its small open area surrounded by conifers. From the summit, Owls Head Pond is seen immediately below, and there are good views of Raquette Lake and Forked Lake to the southwest. The hazy summit of Blue Mountain is seen just east of south, while Kempshall Mountain looms ahead in the distance. The 14 miles of Long Lake itself, so close by, are mostly hidden from view.

Trail in winter: Because of steepness of the terrain in the last half mile, snowshoes are preferable to skis.

Pillsbury Mountain

Round-trip Distance: 3.2 mi (5.1 km)
Elevation Change: 1337 ft (408 m)
Summit Elevation: 3597 ft (1096 m)
Difficulty: (3) A strenuous climb over a moderate
                            distance.
Maps: ADK Central Region map (D-1) or
                            Page Mt. 7.5' and West Canada Lakes 7.5'

Pillsbury Mountain is a moderately difficult climb that makes a good day trip. There is a fire tower at the summit, but the cab is closed. Although there are no views from the ground, a full-circle view is available by climbing to the upper landings of the tower.

▶ Trailhead: Access to the trail is off NY 30 at Mason Lake. The lake is 8.1 mi north of Speculator and 4.0 mi south of the bridge over Lewey Lake outlet. Coming from the south, turn left (right if coming from Lewey Lake) on the excellent Perkins Clearing Road, driving southwest past Mason Lake to the road junction at Perkins Clearing (3.3 mi). Note that this road is closed from December 1 to May 1.

The condition of the road from this point varies considerably with the season and depending on whether lumbering operations are taking place. Be sure your vehicle is in good operating condition. A careful driver should be able to travel this route in summer without much trouble.

Turn right at the Perkins Clearing DEC trail sign. The road passes a metal gate at 3.4 mi, and the bridge over the Miami River is at 4.6 mi. (The old Miami River lean-to was located on the left, just beyond the bridge. It was removed after the Perkins Clearing

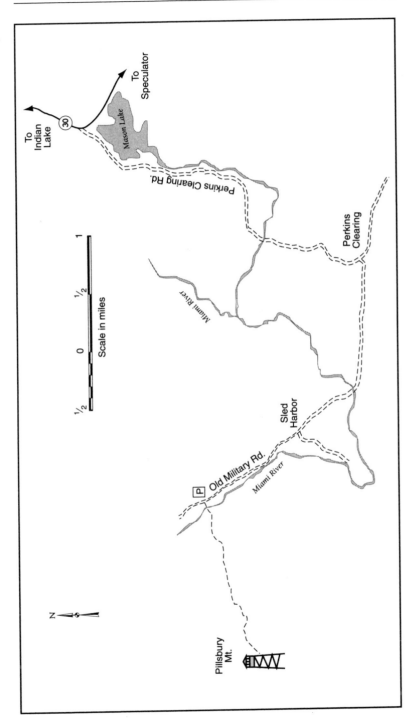

land exchange of 1979.) Sled Harbor is reached at 5.1 mi. At one time, wagons were replaced at this point and oxen were used to pull sleds up the grades ahead. Today, the area is used as a collecting and storing point for logs, and considerable activity with hauling trucks sometimes takes place here.

The route beyond this point is still more difficult and requires good driving skills. Some drivers elect to leave their low-clearance cars at Sled Harbor and walk the rest of the way to the trail, only 1.1 mi farther. Beyond Sled Harbor, one drives up a short grade and immediately takes the side road to the right, "Old Military Road" on old maps. Ascend at a moderate grade. Difficulty of this section varies, depending on recent rainfall and maintenance. The grade and road soon improve, then steepen moderately again at 6.2 mi. The trailhead parking area and road barrier are reached at 6.3 mi. The parking lot holds 10–15 vehicles.

The Pillsbury trailhead is immediately to the left of the trail register at the rear of the parking area. ◄

The trail immediately descends 0.1 mi westward, crossing the Miami River, which is a small brook at this point. Once across the stream, climbing begins in earnest. The grade varies from moderate to steep for the next 1.0 mi. After passing through minor blowdown, the trail finally levels a bit at 1.1 mi.

At 1.3 mi an indistinct trail junction is found at the base of the last steep rock area before the summit. A side trail to the right leads 200 yards to a spring. It has been little used since the fire tower was abandoned and is thus in poor condition. Once past the last steep section, the nearly level trail leads to the fire tower and cabin at 1.6 mi.

Views from the fire tower's upper landings are striking. Snowy Mountain is seen to the north with Indian Lake to its east and Cedar River Flow to its west. Westward from the tower is the West Canada Lakes Wilderness. Pillsbury and Whitney Lakes are in the foreground, while the Cedar Lakes are visible in the distance beyond Pillsbury Lake. Lake Pleasant and Sacandaga Lake are to the south. Mountains, including the vast bulk of Crane Mountain, dominate the distant horizon to the east.

Trail in winter: Pillsbury Mountain is an excellent snowshoeing mountain. However, the access roads are often closed in winter, and the round-trip distance from Mason Lake is 15.8 mi.

Poke-O-Moonshine Mountain

Round-trip Distance: 2.4 mi (3.8 km)
Elevation Change: 1280 ft (390 m)
Summit Elevation: 2180 ft (664 m)
Difficulty: (3) A short hike, but steep sections in the first half.
Maps: Ausable Forks 7.5'

This fire tower peak is extremely popular because of its expansive view of the Lake Champlain Valley and Green Mountains of Vermont to the east and the high peaks in the distance to the southwest. Its unusual name appears to be a combination of two Algonquin Indian words, "pohqui" and "moosie," which mean, respectively, "broken" and "smooth." The name, which was later corrupted by the early settlers, seems to refer to the smooth rocks of the summit or the prominent slab on the southeast side and the broken rocks of the impressive 1000-foot cliffs on the east side.

These accessible rocks in the northeast corner of the Adirondacks and Poke-O-Moonshine's shape, height, and geology make it a premier Adirondack site for rock climbing. Climbers have identified more than 180 routes up the cliffs, taking advantage of their many cracks, sills, and ledges. The rock is mainly gneiss, a metamorphic silt formed over 1.1 billion years ago. One easily observes an onion-like peeling of the rock, a phenomenon geologists call "exfoliation." This peeling is enhanced when water seeps into cracks in the rock, then expands as it freezes, pushing the rock apart.

The first observation station was built on Poke-O-Moonshine in 1912. It was replaced in 1917 with the standardized steel tower seen there today. The tower was deactivated in 1988; the number of fires had decreased with the maturing forest, and spotting smoke and fire from light aircraft proved easier and cheaper. Over succeeding years, the tower became unsuitable for safe climbing.

In 1997, a group of tower restoration enthusiasts formed the Friends of Poke-O-Moonshine, a partnership among nearby chapters of the Adirondack Mountain Club, the town of Chesterfield, local businesses, the NYS Department of Environmental Conservation, and hundreds of individuals. The Friends also operates in partnership with and under the financial auspices of Adirondack Architectural Heritage (AARCH), the regional not-for-profit historic preservation organization. The fire tower at the summit has received extensive restoration by the Friends, with more work to be done in 2001. The trail to the summit is a self-guided nature walk.

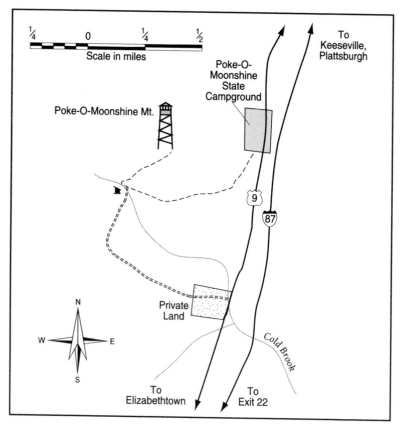

Interpretive pamphlets are available at the trailhead. For more information about the Friends of Poke-O-Moonshine, see Appendix A.

▶ Trailhead: The trail starts at the state campground on Rt. 9, 9.3 mi north of the junction of the road from Lewis to exit 32 on the Northway and 3.0 mi south of exit 33. There is a parking fee at the state campground (and all similar facilities), and parking on the highway in front of the campground is prohibited. Hikers should either be prepared to pay this fee or to walk a few hundred yards extra from outside the "no parking" zone. ◀

Starting from the south end of the campground, the red-marked trail enters the woods and immediately begins climbing, steeply at times, to the base of a cliff at 0.3 mi. Skirting the cliff on the left, the trail switchbacks to a good lookout on the right at 0.1 mi farther. The grade now eases somewhat but remains steady to a saddle south of the summit at 0.8 mi. Here are the remains of the fire observer's cabin, with a lean-to approximately 65 yards to the left.

From this saddle, there are two trails leading up to the right. The trail on the left is now marked as the official route; it leads past a lookout on the left and along a shelf before turning right and up to the summit plateau. The summit has excellent views from ground level to the east and west, but, a 360° panorama is only available from the fire tower, restored in July 2001 by six volunteers from the Student Conservation Association's AmeriCorps program working in cooperation with DEC. Continued maintenance will be needed. See Appendix A for the DEC contact.

Trail in winter: Snowshoes recommended rather than skis, due to steepness of the terrain.

Snowy Mountain

Round-trip Distance:	7.8 mi (12.5 km)
Elevation Change:	2106 ft (642 m)
Summit Elevation:	3899 ft (1188 m)
Difficulty:	(3) A long ascent; steep and rocky in the middle.
Maps:	ADK Central Region map (A, B-2) or Indian Lake 7.5'

Snowy Mountain is an imposing giant west of NY 30 near Indian Lake. It lacks being a 4000-ft peak by only 101 ft. The climbing ascent is 2106 ft, which is greater than that of many of the High Peaks. The summit has excellent views from ground level to the east and west, but, a 360° panorama is only available from the fire tower, restored in July 2001 by six volunteers from the Student Conservation Association's AmeriCorps program working in cooperation with DEC. Continued maintenance will be needed. See Appendix A for the DEC contact.

▶ Trailhead: Access to the trailhead is off the west side of NY 30, 7.3 mi south of Indian Lake village and 17.4 mi north of Speculator. A well-marked parking area is located on the east side of the road, opposite the trailhead. ◀

The trail is marked with red DEC trail markers. It heads west up Beaver Brook Valley on a fairly level track, gaining only 267 ft in elevation before crossing Beaver Brook at 1.2 mi. A steep section, followed by a more gradual section, occurs before Beaver Brook is again crossed at 1.9 mi, another 180 ft higher. The trail has opened up.

The stream and several tributaries are crossed as steady climb-

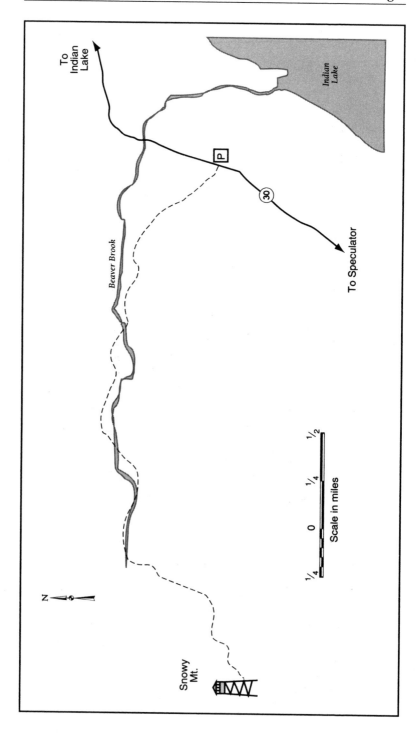

ing begins. Severe erosion is evident as the route steepens. There is a good lookout toward the east at 3.2 mi. Climbing is extremely steep from the lookout to the summit.

A tower affords splendid views of all the mountains of the central Adirondacks. On a clear day, the High Peaks can be spotted to the northeast, beyond and right of prominent Blue Mountain due north.

Several flights of stairs and the floor of the cab are missing from the fire tower, so no access to the tower is possible. However, a side trail extends 50 yards west of the spring to a lookout toward Squaw and Panther Mountains. Even Mt. Morris, near Tupper Lake, can be seen beyond Panther.

Trail in winter: This is a popular snowshoe trail in winter. Its 2016-foot vertical ascent and very steep upper slopes require the same skills and equipment used for winter climbs in the High Peaks.

Vanderwhacker Mountain

Round-trip Distance:	5.4 mi (8.6 km)
Elevation Change:	1650 ft (503 m)
Summit Elevation:	3385 ft (1032 m)
Difficulty:	(3) Level over first half, then relentlessly steep.
Maps:	ADK High Peaks Region map (H-7) or Newcomb 7.5'

The summits of Vanderwhacker and Goodnow Mountains provide perhaps the finest panoramas of the High Peaks to be seen from the southern Adirondacks. The 1918 Aermotor fire tower on Vanderwhacker is in good condition, due to restoration work by DEC, AmeriCorps volunteers, and the Friends of Vanderwhacker Fire Tower.

▶ Trailhead: Access to the trailhead is on a gravel road off the west side of NY 28N, immediately north of the Boreas River bridge. There is a signpost at the junction. The initial grade from the highway is on loose hardscrabble stone, but the road is satisfactory beyond this point if speed is controlled. Avoid a left turn at 1.5 mi just before crossing Vanderwhacker Brook on a bridge. Several open campsites and fireplaces are found in this area. The abandoned D&H Railroad is crossed and the road narrows noticeably. A junction is reached at 2.6 mi; the Vanderwhacker Mountain route bears right. (Continuing left past this junction leads to the private Moose Club, which is not open to the public.) A small sign indicating the

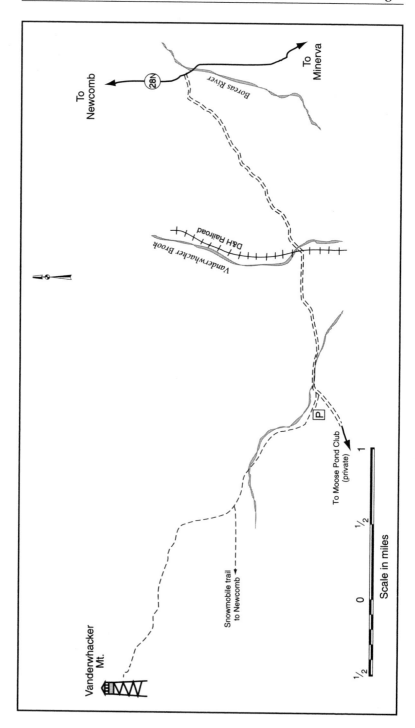

trailhead direction may be seen. The trailhead and parking area are soon reached. ◄

The wide trail, with red DEC hiking trail and snowmobile trail markers, climbs gradually northwest through a hardwood forest. Soon leveling off, it swings north along the left bank of a brook, which it crosses on a wide bridge at 0.3 mi.

A beaver dam on the right at 0.6 mi has flooded the trail, forcing its relocation to the left. A long marsh is on the left at 0.7 mi, with Little Beaver Mountain visible in the distant west. The hiking trail weaves in and out of the snowmobile route as it follows the edge of the marsh. At 0.9 mi, a second beaver dam can be seen on the left and the trail begins to climb away from the marsh.

The snowmobile trail turns left at 1.3 mi, bearing around the base of the mountain, while the hiking trail continues straight ahead. The grade becomes moderate just before the fire observer's cabin is reached at 1.4 mi. The trail traverses a large yard, covered with grass and berry bushes, to the cabin and outbuildings.

The trail continues uphill between the buildings, the slope becoming moderate and then steep. At 1.8 mi, the grade eases appreciably as it passes through a small hollow. The remaining distance to the summit at 2.7 mi is extremely attractive with gradual upgrades.

The summit is closed in on three sides, but magnificent open views can be obtained to the north. Algonquin Peak and Avalanche Pass stand out. Mounts Colden, Redfield, Marcy, Haystack, Allen, Gothics, Sawteeth, Nipple Top, Dix, and Macomb, as well as the Boreas Range and many minor peaks, can be seen. A 360° view is gained from the fire tower. Moose Pond is below to the south. Beaver Ponds and Split Rock Pond are more distant in the southwest.

Trail in winter: The access road is not plowed in winter and is excellent for skiing to the caretaker cabin. The skier had best then switch to snowshoes for the steep ascent to the summit.

Wakely Mountain

Round-trip Distance:	6.0 mi (9.6 km)
Elevation Change:	1635 ft (498 m)
Summit Elevation:	3744 ft (1141 m)
Difficulty:	(3) Level over first half, then steep and challenging.
Maps:	ADK Central Region map (A-1) or Indian Lake 7.5' and Wakely Mountain 7.5'

Wakely is only 256 ft short of being a 4000-ft peak. The climber ascends 1194 ft in the last 1.1 mi. The 70-ft fire tower, second tallest in the Forest Preserve, has ten flights of stairs to its observation cab. Much of the tower is above tree level, affording a 360° view.

▶ Trailhead: Access is via Cedar River Road. Drive along Cedar River Road 11.6 mi to the trailhead sign on the left. Turn right down the narrow gravel lane 0.1 mi to a parking area. A DEC register is here. A drive 0.3 mi farther along Cedar River Road brings you to Wakely Dam, where swimming, camping, and canoeing are possible. ◀

From the trailhead, walk northwest along a gravel road. The red DEC trail markers are seldom seen. A brief view of the summit can be had at 0.3 mi. The remains of an old lumber camp are found over a bank to the left at 0.7 mi. Pass by a side road on the right and then cross a stream on a bridge at 1.1 mi. The route parallels the stream for a short time before veering away.

Two more streams are crossed before a sign on the right at 1.9 mi points to a footpath to the Wakely Mountain tower. (Before making this turn, note the clearing straight ahead, the site of an old beaver pond, worth a brief visit.)

Turn right and climb the steep trail to the summit. Yellow and red markers are intermixed on the ascent, and unmarked trails branch off the main trail at several points. A side trail to the right leads to a helipad site 80 yds from the fire tower clearing.

The summit fire tower is reached at 3.0 mi. Ground views can be had only to the southeast toward Cedar River Flow. Full-circle observation is possible from the fire tower, with Snowy Mountain to the southeast and Blue Mountain to the north. The lake country opens up to the west.

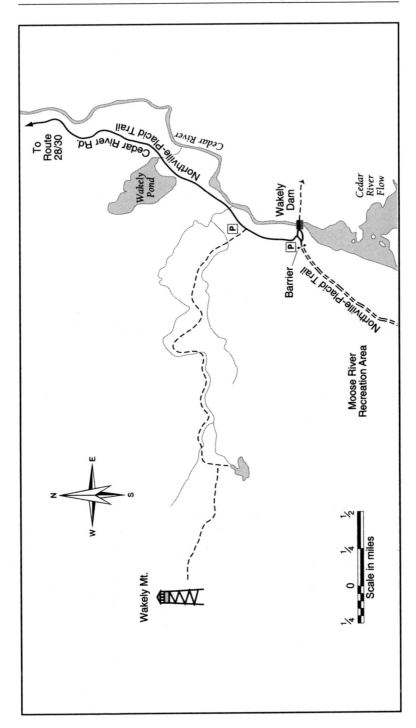

M. Clark

The 70-ft fire tower atop Wakely Mountain, second highest standing tower in the Adirondack Park. The highest tower in New York State at 100 feet was constructed on Swancott Hill on the Tug Hill Plateau. It has since been removed.

Trail in winter: Wakely Mountain is a short but rugged snowshoe climb in winter. However, the more serious obstacle is that from December to April, Cedar River Road is plowed from NY 28/30 only to a point 4.6 mi from the trailhead. Beyond that point, the road is a winter snowmobile route. Inquire locally for a snowmobile ride. If skis are used for the 4.6 mi along this road, they can also be used on the first 1.9 mi of the trail before they need to be traded for snowshoes.

Woodhull Mountain

Round-trip Distance: 15.2 mi (24.3 km)
Elevation Change: 812 ft (247 m)
Summit Elevation: 2362 ft (720 m)
Difficulty: (3) Strenuous, only because of distance; level over first five miles and steep ascent only near the end.
Maps: ADK West-Central Region map (B-5) or Honnedaga Lake 7.5', McKeever 7.5', and Thendara 7.5'

The steel tower on this summit dates from 1916. The 7.6-mi access route traverses Black River Wild Forest lands, and thus lends itself to quicker passage in summer by using a mountain bike the first five miles along the route of an old railroad bed, leaving only about 2.5 mi. to be hiked on foot.

▶ Trailhead: Driving south on NY 28 from Old Forge, turn left just south of the Moose River bridge on McKeever Road. Go 0.3 mi to a junction. The pavement turns left; leave it and continue straight ahead on a dirt road past the old railroad station. Cross the tracks and continue to the second parking lot 0.8 mi from the highway. (The first parking lot, on the right, is for the Wolf Lake Landing Road.)

Driving north from Utica on NY 12 and 28, bear right on NY 28 at Alder Creek. Proceed 17 mi farther to McKeever and the right turn onto McKeever Road. See McKeever Road above for remaining directions. ◀

Starting from the second parking lot and trail register, the route continues beyond the barricade on a surprisingly smooth surface. This rebuilt roadway follows the roadbed of the former Moose River Lumber Company railroad, which went to #4 camp near Woodhull Mountain. You may notice the gentle slope of the route, and the occasional cut needed to avoid sudden climbs. (This first section of the route, about 5 mi, makes a good mountain bike or ski approach.)

At 0.7 mi, a trail right leads to Bear Lake and beyond. At 2.6 mi, a yellow route crossing the trail leads left (north) 0.5 mi to Remsen Falls and right (south) to Woodhull Lake via the Wolf Lake Landing Road.

Little visited, Woodhull Mountain tower sits 7.6 mi into the forest near Old Forge.

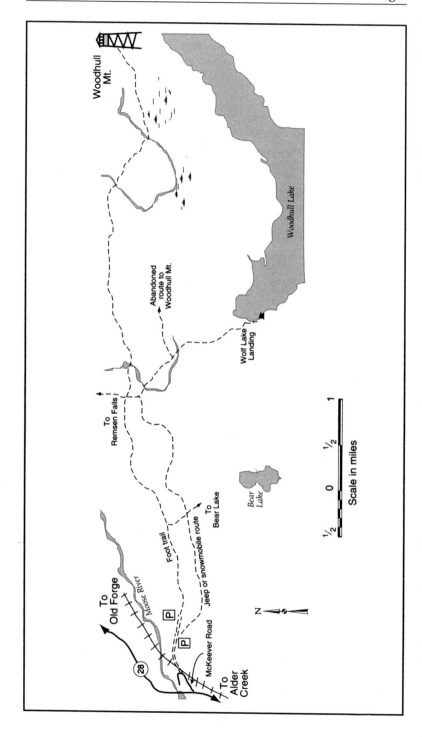

Continuing ahead to the east, the Woodhull Mountain Trail passes a small pond on the left at 2.9 mi. After some gentle climbing, the route levels off. It was in this area that the logging railroad crew headed for #4 camp would unhook the moving cars from the engine and race ahead to pull off to the left on a Y. After the cars rolled by on the main line, they would back the engine on the second leg of the Y, rejoin the main line going in reverse, catch up with the cars, and hook on before applying the brakes at #4 camp. The train was thus arranged for the return trip. As it starts down the gentle slope, the road finally leaves the railroad bed and turns slightly left. You can see the remains of the old railroad bed continuing on ahead.

The road seems to rejoin the railroad route a short distance farther on, but the route becomes slightly rougher and finally ends in a sharp right turn on a creek bank at 5.1 mi. Turn left at the end of the road, on the creek bottom, and cross over the creek. The route continues from the creek bank as a narrow foot trail, fairly well marked with a combination of red DEC markers, red painted can lids, red tape, and finally orange and red rectangular markers. From here on, the trail climbs steadily, with very few level parts.

At 5.6 mi, a red-marked hunters' trail goes right, and the trail turns sharply left. The route climbs more steeply and zigzags somewhat randomly. It drops into a swampy creek bed at 6.1 mi, climbs steeply for a short distance, and reaches a trail junction at 6.4 mi. (The route straight ahead shows the heaviest use. This, too, is a hunters' trail, marked occasionally with red paint blazes, that leads 0.3 mi to the Wolf Lake Landing Road Extension.)

The red DEC trail turns left and continues climbing. A creek at 6.6 mi provides a brief level section, followed by more climbing through thicket and blowdown. As the trail levels out, it becomes bumpier and somewhat overgrown, finally leading to the fire tower near a huge boulder at 7.6 mi.

The only view from the ground may be obtained by going east on the summit for 200 ft to the site of a burned cabin, where a limited opening to the east gives a glimpse of unending forest and hills. A better view by far can be gained by climbing the tower, which is open to just below the cab. To the south, one can see part of Woodhull Lake, with Big Island visible at the near end. Atop the dam at the far end, look for the nineteenth century valve house that regulates the reservoir's outflow to Woodhull Creek, the Black River, and ultimately to the New York State barge canal at Rome. To the north, Nicks Lake is visible. Beyond the valley of the Old Forge–Inlet chain of lakes (only specks of water visible), is Bald

Adirondack Park Fire Towers That May Not Last

Mount Adams

Round-trip Distance:	4.8 mi (7.7 km)
Elevation Change:	1800 ft (549 m)
Summit Elevation:	3540 ft (1080 m)
Difficulty:	(4) Large elevation gain; trail steep in places.
Maps:	ADK High Peaks Region map (C-11) or Santanoni Peak 7.5'

The 47-ft Aermotor steel tower on this peak dates from 1917. It was abandoned in 1972 and until recently (2004) was in poor condition. There are practically no views from the summit without access to the tower. With the 2005 purchase of the Tahawus tract, by the Open Space Institute from NL Industries for eventual transfer to the NYS Department of Environmental Conservation, some

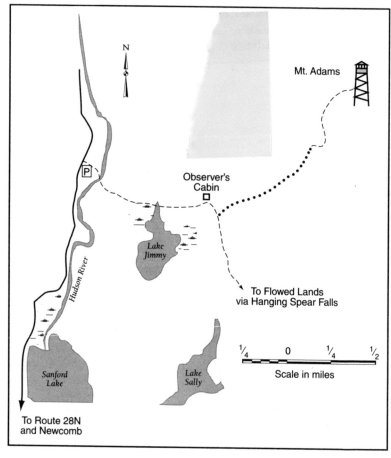

maintenance work has been allowed by OSI. DEC has had restoration materials airlifted to the summit and is supervising AmeriCorps volunteers from the Student Conservation Association in making tower repairs. In short, the future looks brighter for the Adams tower, and its survival is more likely than has been expressed in previous printings of this guidebook. ADK is on record as supporting its retention by agreement between OSI and the state.

The hiking trail from the Hanging Spear Falls trail to the summit, though recently obscure and hard to follow, also received attention in 2005 from AmeriCorps workers and should be redesigned and rerouted eventually to avoid the steepest sections.

▶ Trailhead: The parking lot for the Hanging Spear Falls Trail serves as the trailhead for Mount Adams. Access to this lot is from Rt. 28N, at a point about 5 mi east of the Newcomb Town Hall and 14 mi north of Minerva. Turn north on the road to Tahawus. About 6 mi from Rt. 28N, the road forks, with the main road continuing across a bridge over the Hudson River to the Tahawus open-pit mine. Turn left here on the narrower road marked with a sign to "Marcy and the High Peaks." The road passes a large stone iron furnace 2.8 mi from the fork. At 3.0 mi, turn right into the parking lot for the Hanging Spear Falls Trail, which leads to Flowed Lands. ◀

The route to Mount Adams begins by hiking 0.8 mi along the yellow-marked Hanging Spear Falls Trail. A few hundred yards from the old observer's cabin, the Mount Adams Trail diverges left. The Mount Adams Trail was once marked with red DEC markers, but they are now difficult to locate. The trail ascends at first at an easy grade and then at moderate to very steep grades to the summit.

Trail in winter: Toward the top, this route is too steep for skis, but snowshoers may enjoy the challenge.

Hurricane Mountain

There are three approaches to this popular rocky summit. Use of multiple vehicles provides an opportunity for through hikes. Hurricane offers one of the most commanding views of any of the lesser peaks, and as a result it was an important survey station for Verplanck Colvin during his Adirondack survey. For many years there was an active fire tower on the peak, but the tower has been abandoned and condemned. It is classed as "nonconforming," and may be removed entirely in the near future. (See preface for a fuller discussion of this point.) The view from the ground encompasses much of the length of Lake Champlain and the Green Mountains in Vermont, as well as many of the High Peaks. Blueberries are plentiful starting in early August.

Hurricane Mountain from Rt. 9N

Round-trip Distance:	5.2 mi (8.3 km)
Elevation Change:	2000 ft (610 m)
Summit Elevation:	3694 ft (1126 m)
Difficulty:	(3) A strenuous climb with steep sections for a fairly long distance.
Maps:	ADK High Peaks Region map (G-6, 7) or Elizabethtown 7.5', Keene Valley 7.5', Lake Placid 7.5', and Lewis 7.5'

This is the most heavily used of the three approaches to the summit.

▶ Trailhead: This trail leaves the north side of Rt. 9N at the height of land 3.6 mi east of the junction of Rtes. 9N and 73 between Keene and Keene Valley and 6.8 mi. west of the junction of Rtes. 9N and 9 at the southern end of the village of Elizabethtown. On the south side of Rt. 9N, opposite the trailhead, is a small parking lot. ◀

Marked with red DEC disks, the trail leaves the highway, following a tote road. At first it climbs steeply but soon levels off and becomes a footpath at 0.3 mi. The trail continues nearly on the level through mostly thick conifers as it crosses a series of small brooks

Abandoned Hurricane Mountain tower, a "nonconforming stucture"(winter 2000)

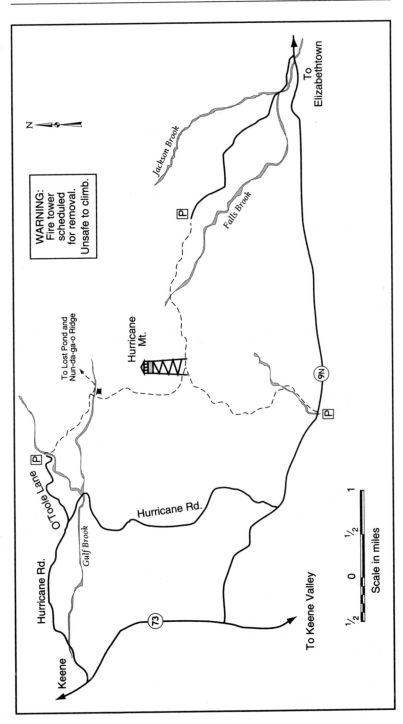

and bog bridges built by ADK volunteer and professional trail crews. Crossing the last stream at 1.1 mi, the trail heads into hardwood forest and begins to climb steadily. The first of several steep pitches begins at 1.7 mi, and the trail alternates between steep and easy climbing to the crest of the ridge and the junction with the ADK trail from Keene at 2.5 mi. Turning right, the trail soon climbs up over the summit rocks and reaches the summit at 2.6 mi.

Trail in winter: This is ideal on snowshoes, although rigorous.

Hurricane Mountain from the East

Round-trip Distance: 5.4 mi (8.6 km)
Elevation Change: 1700 ft (518 m)
Summit Elevation: 3694 ft (1126 m)
Difficulty: (3) A strenuous climb with steep sections for a fairly long distance.
Maps: ADK High Peaks Region map (G-6, 7) or Elizabethtown 7.5', Keene Valley 7.5', Lake Placid 7.5', and Lewis 7.5'

This approach was once used by the fire tower observer and was the shortest route to the summit, but as of 1998 a landowner has closed the road to vehicular traffic at a point 1.2 mi below the former observer's cabin. This approach is now about the same length as the trail from Rt. 9N. A lean-to once located just beyond the observer's cabin site has been removed. Because of this closure, the DEC may soon discontinue maintenance on the trail, although it will remain a legal foot access to state land.

▶ Trailhead: The start is at the end of a dirt road that branches right off Rt. 9N 2.2 mi from the junction of Rtes. 9N and 9 at the southern end of the village of Elizabethtown. The road turns right just before a bridge and climbs steadily to a gate blocking further vehicular access at 2.7 mi, where there is a small parking area on the right. Parking is not permitted on the road. ◀

From the gate, proceed up the road to the site of the former observer's cabin at the end of the road at 1.2 mi. Past this point, the trail drops down a few yards to a stream. The trail then begins climbing moderately, but after crossing another stream at 1.4 mi, it climbs steeply with only a few breathers until it emerges on the rocks just before reaching the summit at 2.7 mi.

Trail in winter: This route is ideal on snowshoes, although rigorous.

Hurricane Mountain via the North Trail

Round-trip Distance: 6.0 mi (9.6 km)
Elevation Change: 1600 ft (488 m)
Summit Elevation: 3694 ft (1126 m)
Difficulty: (3) A strenuous climb with steep sections for a fairly long distance.
Maps: ADK High Peaks Region map (G-6, 7) or Elizabethtown 7.5', Keene Valley 7.5', Lake Placid 7.5', and Lewis 7.5'

This is the longest approach to Hurricane, but the grades are moderate throughout. There is an attractive and little-used lean-to just over a mile from the end of the road, which makes this approach a wonderful first camping trip for families with young children. The trail is marked with ADK markers and maintained by the Hurricane Mountain Chapter of ADK.

▶ Trailhead: From just south of the center of the hamlet of Keene, proceed east 2.3 mi on Hurricane Road up a long hill. Just past the Mountain House, bear left on O'Toole Lane where East Hill Road makes a sharp right turn. This point can also be reached by following Hurricane Road approximately 4.0 mi north from Rt. 9N. Proceed up the dirt road 1.2 mi to its end at Crow Clearing, where cars may be parked. ◀

Leaving the right side of the clearing, the Hurricane Trail crosses a bridge over a small brook, crosses another small stream at 0.4 mi, and continues mostly on the level to Gulf Brook Lean-to at 1.1 mi, where an ADK trail bears left to Lost Pond.

Turning sharply right in front of the lean-to, the Hurricane Trail crosses Gulf Brook and begins a gradual to moderate ascent. At 1.2 mi the trail crosses a small brook, which it recrosses several more times before finally ending up on the right bank at 1.2 mi. Veering left, the trail now climbs at a steady, moderate grade through a beautiful birch forest to the junction with the trail from Rt. 9N (see above) at 2.8 mi. Continuing straight ahead, the trail soon reaches the summit rocks and then the summit at 3.0 mi.

Trail in winter: This is the only one of the three routes that is practical on backcountry skis. Snowshoes work, too.

Lyon Mountain

Round-trip Distance: 5.0 mi (8 km)
Elevation Change: 1790 ft (546 m)
Summit Elevation: 3830 ft (1167 m)
Difficulty: (3) Steep for much of the climb; a rigorous High Peak-type trail.
Maps: Moffitsville 7.5'

This trail climbs a massive isolated peak in the far northeastern area of the Adirondack Park to offer what few mountains in the Adirondacks can—a truly international view. Red-marked, it is the only DEC-designated trail in the scattered patches of Forest Preserve in the immediate area, but until recently the tower and trail actually lay on the property of Domtar Industries, a timber company.

In January, 2005, Domtar sold 20,000 acres of its holdings around Lyon Mt. to The Nature Conservancy (TNC) for eventual re-sale to New York State. TNC and the Adirondack Mountain Club are collaborating to redesign the trail, and some work by DEC to recondition the tower began in 2005, with more work envisioned in 2006.

▶ Trailhead: Access to this trail is obtained by taking NY 374 west from Interstate 87 (the Adirondack Northway) at Exit 38N near Plattsburgh. Follow Rt. 374 for approximately 23.2 mi over Dannemora Mountain and around Chazy Lake, above which Lyon Mountain looms, to the Chazy Lake Road. For those coming from the west, this intersection is 3.7 mi. east of the center of Lyon Mountain village. Turn south on the Chazy Lake Road and proceed 1.8 mi to a gravel road on the right. Take this gravel road 0.9 mi to its end at the white ruins of the Lowenberg Ski Area lodge. Park here; the trail begins to the left of the lodge ruins. ◀

The trail starts its steady, strenuous ascent to the 3,830-ft peak of Lyon Mountain by initially following an old jeep road through a second-growth forest of aspen and cherry. This area was clear-cut about a quarter century ago for a ski trail. The forest had been cut over heavily to furnish charcoal for iron smelting in the last century.

At 1.0 mi, you begin to see balsam fir. Shortly thereafter, at 1.1 mi, keep left at an intersection; the right fork goes to the top of the old ski slope. White birch begins to appear at 1.2 mi and at 1.3 mi the remains of the old fire observer's cabin are seen.

The trail continues rising steeply, keeping right at another fork where the telephone wire path goes to the left. The forest is now composed of mature white birch with an undergrowth of spruce and fir. The spruce and fir indicate the composition of the future forest here, while the white birch attest to the severe forest fires that occurred at the turn of the century.

At 1.8 mi balsam fir becomes the dominant tree in the canopy as the winds begin to pick up somewhat. Deer come up to this zone

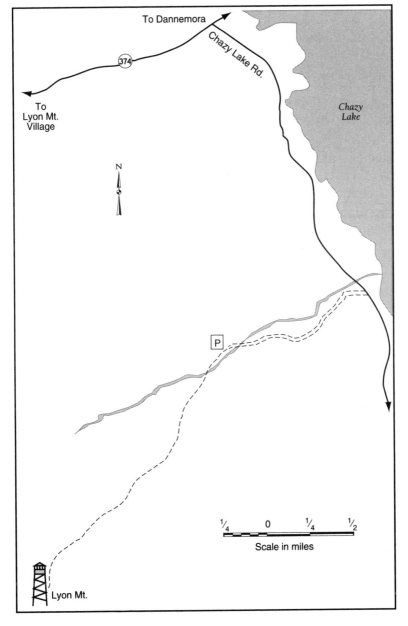

in the summer to use the increased wind velocity to escape the biting flies down below.

The summit is reached at 2.5 mi, following an unusually steep pitch. The steel fire tower dates from 1917 and will soon be restored. The summit is covered with scrubby conifers and mountain ash, as is also the case on the summits of DeBar and St. Regis Mountains. This vegetation is an indication of the poor soil and harsh climatic conditions on the exposed tops of these mountains. The craggy slopes of Ellenburg and Johnson Mountains can be seen nearby, while the distant High Peaks may be seen to the south on a clear day. That same clear day can also provide a view of the skyscrapers in Montreal. Closer by, both the St. Lawrence River and Lake Champlain can be seen, with the Green Mountains of Vermont clearly outlined to the east.

Trail in winter: The trail makes a reasonable snowshoe trip, but is too steep for cross-country skiing.

Spruce Mountain

Round-trip Distance:	2.2 mi (3.5 km)
Elevation Change:	1003 ft (306 m)
Summit Elevation:	2003 ft (611 m)
Difficulty:	(2) A short and moderate climb.
Maps:	Corinth 7.5' and Porter Corners 7.5'

Spruce Mountain is a good choice for those who like to climb mountains that don't require much work. (Belfry Mountain is an even shorter hike. See p. 51.) The summit can be reached by a trail along the route of an old jeep road that is intersected by numerous logging roads. There is also a gated service road that is closed to the driving public but could be walked, although the distance is about twice that of the trail. Climbing this mountain requires attention to the trail route to avoid wandering onto a side trail. Its summit is interesting, with three radio antennas, a microwave tower, a generator, and an abandoned 73-ft fire tower that is in disrepair and not recommended for climbing. This tower, the highest remaining in the Forest Preserve, begs restoration.

Please note that although this trail is a marked hiking trail, it traverses International Paper Company lands that have been leased to the Magoo Hunt Club and the Blue Jay Club. The Blue Jays and Magoos frown on hikers during big game hunting season. It is recommended that hikers refrain from using this area during deer season.

▶ Trailhead: Take NY 9N south from Corinth and turn sharply right (west) on Wells Road 1.0 mi south of the second railroad crossing.

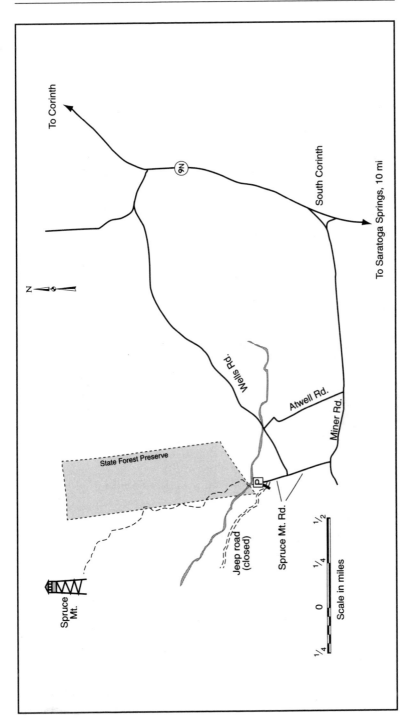

Drive 2.0 mi until Wells Road intersects Spruce Mountain Road.
Turn right and drive another 0.2 mi to the end of the road and a
gravel parking circle.

From the south, drive north on NY 9N from Saratoga Springs
for 10 mi. At the settlement at South Corinth, turn left on Miner
Road. Travel west for about 1.5 mi, then right on Wells Road. Where
Wells Road forks right, continue straight ahead on Spruce Mountain Road to the trailhead. ◀

The trail begins at the far end of the circle by crossing a fast-
flowing stream that runs through a large culvert. Bearing right,
it proceeds as a continuation of the road, which is now an old
washed-out jeep trail, although it shows evidence of a substantial
amount of use in days gone by.

In about 70 yds the trail bears left up a steep foot path marked
by a DEC sign on a post. In another 25 yds it intersects an abandoned road. The route turns left, uphill. The trail up this old road
leads north almost continuously uphill to the summit, marked in-
termittently by red DEC disks.

At 0.2 mi an old logging road enters from the right. At 0.2 mi,
POSTED signs (Magoo Hunt Club) and orange surveyor tape around
trees indicate the boundary between state land and private holdings. Another old road branches right here, but the trail continues
straight ahead.

The trail climbs steadily, but moderately. At 0.4 mi it curves to
the right again, climbing through open forests of birch, beech, oak,
and other hardwoods, with groves of moderately-sized hemlocks
adding their beauty to the scene. At 0.6 mi, posted signs of the
Blue Jay Club appear on both sides of the trail. Just 23 yds beyond,
another old road crosses the trail from left uphill to right, but the
trail continues north, straight ahead, marked by a small rock cairn.

The road/trail commences a series of brief curves until reaching
a well-marked shortcut. A bright yellow plastic triangle, a blue
painted disk, and a red plastic ribbon mark this shortcut as straight
ahead while the road continues around a curve to the right. The
shortcut saves the hiker about a tenth of a mile and makes it easier
to see and access the next shortcut section, which again saves
time by not following the switchback curves in the old road.

In about 150 yds, the shortcut encounters the road again, but
crosses it and continues north, straight up an embankment past
an enormous ash tree, whose diamond-cut trunk is at least 3 ft in
diameter. Old red DEC markers are tacked to both sides of it.

The route continues up the mountain, passing through an open
area at 0.8 mi with some erratic boulders to the right. Continuing

to climb moderately, it passes between the huge trunks of the original forest trees, suggesting what this area must have looked like before lumbering began.

Very shortly, another logging road crosses the trail, but again, the trail continues straight. A wider old road joins on the right. The trail bears left and traverses a more level section before climbing again.

The summit area is reached at 1.1 mi. The fire tower is located in a grove of young hemlocks that were left standing, although a huge section of trees was cut to clear an area for Saratoga County's radio antennas, which now stand in a dense patch of berry bushes.

Since the fire tower observer system in New York State has been abandoned, most of the old towers are being allowed to deteriorate until they become a hazard and must be removed. That day may come for the Spruce Mountain Tower, but interest in a restoration project could save it. The wooden stairs, landings, and floor of the upper cab need replacing with pressure-treated lumber, and the missing windows of the cabin require replacement, preferably with unbreakable polycarbonate panes. Interpretive panels placed on the lower walls of the cab could identify mountains and other landmarks in view.

Unfortunately, it has become necessary to erect communication antennas on many of the mountains of the state, and Spruce Mountain is one of them. They detract from the pristine, wild nature of the hike, but this is one of the prices we pay for progress. Until the tower is restored, enjoy the view north from the ledge to the right of the tower, where Crane Mountain's profile is most prominent.

Trail in winter: This is an easy snowshoe trek. Well-conditioned, excellent skiers may try skiing it, as there are no impossibly steep sections and the old road is nicely graded for the most part.

St. Regis Mountain

Round-trip Distance:	6.8 mi (10.9 km)
Elevation Change:	1266 ft (386 m)
Summit Elevation:	2874 ft (876 m)
Difficulty:	(3) A challenging hike over a well-maintained trail, steep near the end.
Maps:	ADK Northern Region map (M-3) or Saint Regis Mountain 7.5'

This trail makes a relatively short, steep climb to the summit of an isolated northern Adirondack peak with magnificent views in nearly

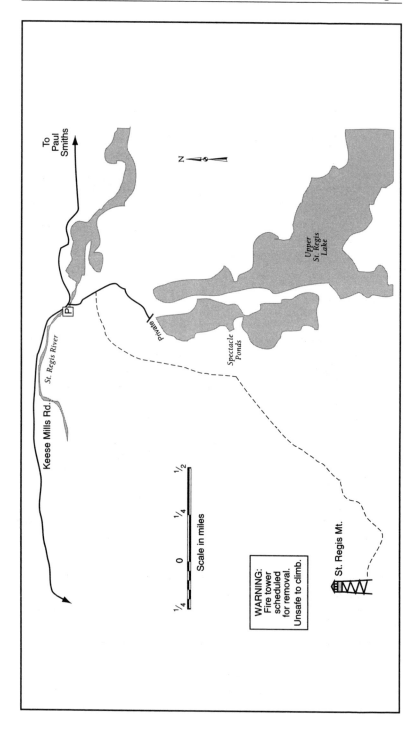

Tower on St. Regis Mountain, soon to be found only in photos

all directions. A closed fire tower dominates the top. Because it is a non-conforming structure in the St. Regis Canoe Area, it is likely to be removed at any time. A new parking area was built in summer 1999, and the first two-thirds of the trail was rebuilt by a professional ADK trail crew working under DEC auspices. It's an interesting reroute which avoids muddy sections and roller-coaster undulations along the boundary of Camp Topridge.

▶ Trailhead: From the main entrance to Paul Smith's College at the intersection of NY 30 and 86, drive north about 200 yds and then turn left (west) on Keese Mills Road. Proceed 2.6 mi to an ample DEC parking lot on the left, just beyond a gravel road leading left to Camp Topridge, the former estate of Marjorie Merriweather Post. Park in the designated parking lot, and not along the private Topridge road. ◀

Leaving the parking lot, walk south down the Topridge road, which immediately crosses the St. Regis River on a narrow metal bridge. At 0.1 mi take the DEC red-marked trail on the right. Sign the trail register, a few yards into the woods. The trail begins an ascent through mature second growth, with brief level sections at 0.2 and 0.4 mi. At 0.6 mi, note the large maple on the left. Switchback sharply left at 0.75 mi and reach a height of land at 1.0 mi in an impressive stand of large hemlocks. The trail now begins a gradual descent, reaches a low point at 1.5 mi and resumes a gradual ascent. At 1.8 mi, a metal pipe and cairn on the left mark the boundary between the Franklin County towns of Brighton and Santa Clara. The intersection with the old trail is reached at 2.2 mi and the trail immediately crosses a perennial brook on a sturdy wooden bridge. Some 35 yds beyond the bridge, a side trail to the left leads 35 yds to an open grassy campsite, the former site of a DEC fire tower observer's cabin.

The main trail soon begins to rise more steeply. Impressive water bars, stepping stones, and rock cribs were constructed by Paul Smith's forestry students. At 3.2 mi, the trail passes enormous boulders. At 3.3 mi, a path to the right leads 20 yds to open bedrock and views westward. The mostly bare summit, dominated by an abandoned fire tower, is gained at 3.4 mi. The bareness of the summit and the presence of white birch attest to earlier clearing by the surveyors under Verplanck Colvin. A few stunted spruce and fir are, as usual, present on the top, along with mountain ash.

The High Peaks, along with McKenzie Mountain and the Seward Range, can be seen to the south. Directly below is a stunning expanse of lakes and ponds within the St. Regis Canoe Area. Eastward, one can see the pointed top of Whiteface with Esther to its left. Slightly to the northeast the isolated peaks of DeBar and Loon Lake Mountains stand out clearly.

Trail in winter: This is a fine summit for snowshoeing, but the steepness of terrain in the last mile will discourage all but the most skillful backcountry skiers.

Catskill Park
Fire Towers

M. Clark

Balsam Lake Mountain

This fire tower summit, sometimes called Balsam Roundtop Mountain, should not be confused with Balsam Mountain to its northeast. Both are located in the western tip of Ulster County.

The first fire tower in New York State was erected on Balsam Lake Mountain in 1887 by the Balsam Lake Club. Built of wood, it survived until 1901 when lightning struck and burned it. In 1905 it was replaced with another wooden tower. Telephone lines, a small observer's cabin, and a road were added in 1909. A steel tower was built in 1919, and replaced by the present steel tower in 1930. Abandonment as a fire lookout in 1988 led to deterioration and removal of the bottom flight of stairs in 1993. Progress in the tower's restoration has moved along in the last two years with help from volunteers in the AmeriCorps program, Boy Scouts, and an ironworkers union, which will be installing replacement bolts and cross braces. A grand reopening took place on June 3, 2000, National Trails Day. For additional information on this project and to help with cabin renovation and continuing tower maintenance, see Appendix A.

Access to the mountain is provided by the Dry Brook Ridge Trail, either from Mill Brook Rd. 3.0 mi to the north or from the end of the Beaver Kill Rd. above Quaker Clearing 1.8 mi to the south. For some hikers, the 3-mile walk from the north may be preferred to the shorter hike from the south owing to easier access to the northern trailhead. A third approach of 6.7 mi, from Alder Lake via the Mill Brook Ridge Trail, offers scenic views and a new lean-to 2.3 mi from the Alder Lake Trailhead.

Balsam Lake Mountain, Northern Approach

Round-trip Distance: 6.0 mi (9.6 km)
Elevation Change: 980 ft (300 m)
Summit Elevation: 3723 ft (1135 m)
Difficulty: (2) A moderate climb with no steep spots.
Maps: Central Catskill Map 42 (G-5, 6)
                         or Arena 7.5' and Seager 7.5'

For those coming from the east and north of the Catskill Park, this approach has the advantage of convenient access to the northern trailhead. Because of heavy use by hunters, it is wise to avoid this trail in deer season. Note that camping is not permitted along the first 2.2 mi of this route, which traverses private land.

▶ Trailhead: From Exits 19 and 20 of the NYS Thruway, drive west via NY 28 or NY 212/28 to Arkville. From the junction of NY 28 and the Dry Brook Road just west of Arkville, drive south on Dry Brook Road (County Rt. 49) through Mapledale (at 4.7 mi) to Stewarts Turn junction at 6.1 mi. Turn right (west) on Mill Brook Road. A height of land is reached in 2.2 mi. The Dry Brook Ridge Trail crosses the road in a north-south direction. Park in the large parking lot on the right (north) side of the road. Farther ahead 0.9 mi, a trailhead and trail on the right leads north 0.25 mi to the Mill Brook lean-to. ◀

From the height of land on Mill Brook Road, the blue-marked Dry Brook Ridge Trail heads to the south and ascends a gradual grade along an unmaintained town road. The upgrade continues to a trail register at 0.15 mi where the trail levels. Alternating climbs and level spots lead to a spring, indicated by a sign and blue-marked side trail, at 1.2 mi. At a height of land at 1.9 mi, a junction with an old road on the left marks the usual departure point for an informal route up Graham Mountain. From here the route gradually descends along the old roadway to a junction with the Balsam Lake Mountain Trail on the right at 2.2 mi. Follow red markers past a barrier up the old jeep road on an easy ascent, reaching the summit and fire tower at 3.0 mi. A picnic table can be found in the small clearing. Views are obscured by trees at ground level, but from the tower, climbers get a breathtaking full-circle view.

Views from the tower unfold spectacularly as you begin to climb above the tree tops. Graham Mountain, 145 ft higher, looms to the east, with its distinctive partner, Doubletop, just behind it to the right. Between these two nearby summits on the far horizon, the Catskills' highest point, Slide Mountain, is visible. Just left of Graham in the distance is Panther Mountain. Closer and farther left to the northeast is a continuous ridgeline that forms the divide between the Hudson and Delaware watersheds; its bumps from right to left are Eagle, Haynes, Balsam, and Belleayre Mountains. Northward, Dry Brook Ridge stretches seven miles north-northeast to Margaretville on the East Branch of the Delaware River. A high ridge of Balsam Lake Mountain (Mill Brook Ridge) extends westward, beyond which a small piece of the Pepacton Reservoir on the East Branch Delaware River is visible. Complex underground aqueducts carry water from this reservoir to New York City. If you have brought binoculars, you may spot the newly painted fire tower on Red Hill to the southeast, with its near twin Denman Mountain to its right.

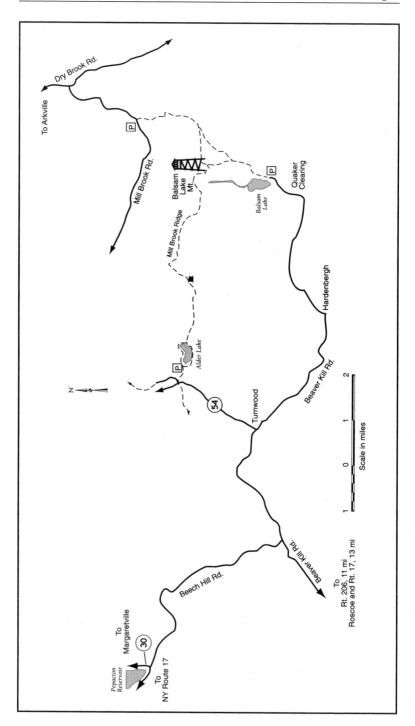

Balsam Lake Mountain Loop, Southern Approach

Round-trip Distance:	4.4 mi (7.0 km)
Elevation Change:	1193 ft (364 m)
Summit Elevation:	3723 ft (1135 m)
Difficulty:	(2) A short hike, with steep ledges.
Maps:	Central Catskill Map 42 (G-6) or Arena 7.5' and Seager 7.5'

For road approach to trailhead, Western Catskill Map 44 or Arena 7.5' and Seager 7.5'.

This hike uses the southern end of the Dry Brook Ridge Trail and all of the 1.6-mi Balsam Lake Mountain Trail. Balsam Lake Mountain can be hiked in conjunction with Graham Mountain to make a fuller day's outing. (See ADK's *Guide to Catskill Trails.*)

▶ Trailhead: Access to the Dry Brook Ridge Trail is from DEC's Balsam Lake Mountain parking area at the end of Beaver Kill Road.

Access from the central Catskills, Kingston, and points north: From the western junction of NY Rts. 28 and 30 about 3 mi southwest of Margaretville (0.0 mi.), continue west on Rt. 30 along the north shore of Pepacton Reservoir, then cross to the south shore. At 10.8 mi, turn left on Beech Hill Road. Proceed uphill, then down again to the junction of Beech Hill Road and Beaver Kill Road at 17.4 mi. Turn left on Beaver Kill Road, driving through the settlements of Turnwood and Quaker Clearing to the road's end at a DEC parking lot at 28.9 mi.

The trailhead can be reached from NY 17 (Exit 94) between Liberty and Hancock. Take NY 206 (County Rt. 7) north from the village of Roscoe traffic light for 2.3 mi to the unmarked Beaver Kill Road on the right. Drive 22.3 mi east on Beaver Kill Road through the village of Beaver Kill's covered bridge and the settlements of Lew Beach, Turnwood, and Hardenbergh, and past Quaker Clearing to the road's end at the DEC parking area 1.2 mi beyond Quaker Clearing. ◀

The blue-marked Dry Brook Ridge Trail heads north-northeast from the parking area trailhead. (Avoid the road that enters the Balsam Lake Anglers Club to the northwest.) It climbs at easy, steady grades before crossing a small stream on an old stone culvert at 0.5 mi. It reaches the Balsam Lake Mountain Trail junction at 0.9 mi, having gained about 400 ft in elevation from the trailhead.

Turn left and follow the red trail markers of the Balsam Lake Mountain Trail to the northwest. The route becomes moderately steep and rocky. At 1.2 mi, the trail veers left to avoid a ledge. At

1.3 mi, a spur trail left leads to the new Balsam Lake Mountain lean-to and privy. A pipe coming from the base of a rock at 1.35 mi marks a spring to the right of the trail. A spur trail leads right to the site of former lean-tos at 1.4 mi. These two lean-tos were removed in 1999 and 2000 from this location at about 3600 ft and replaced by the new single lean-to below 3500 ft.

The Balsam Lake Mountain Trail turns abruptly left from the lean-to junction. The last stretch to the summit clearing seems almost flat. It reaches the Mill Brook Ridge Trail junction on the left at 1.7 mi, which leads 6.7 mi to a trailhead near Alder Lake. (Consider following this yellow-marked trail west 0.1 mi to a fern glade with a wonderful view of the western Catskills. The entire Mill Brook Ridge Trail is described below.) The summit is at 1.8 mi.

The loop trail leaves the summit heading east from the clearing on a jeep road. The gradual downgrade has short steeper pitches. Fine views are found at 2.0 mi, before moderate grades lose elevation quickly. A barrier gate at 2.45 mi is reached with a second junction with the Dry Brook Ridge Trail at 2.5 mi. The unmarked junction for the informal route to Graham Mountain is 0.35 mi. east at the height of land.

Turn right and follow the blue-marked Dry Brook Ridge Trail to the southwest. Gradual grades take you along a dirt roadway to the first junction with the Balsam Lake Mountain Trail at 3.5 mi. It is another 0.9 mi back to the parking area.

Trail in winter: Traverse of the loop trail clockwise, as described above, requires a very steep ascent, best done on snowshoes. Skiers can traverse the loop counterclockwise to the summit, then return by the same route.

Balsam Lake Mountain via the
Mill Brook Ridge Trail from Alder Lake

Round-trip Distance: 13.4 mi (21.4 km)
Elevation Change: 1620 ft (494 m)
Summit Elevation: 3723 ft (1135 m)
Difficulty: (3) A long approach along a new,
                         well-graded trail.
Maps: Central Catskill Map 42 (E, F, G-6)
                         or Arena 7.5' and Seager 7.5'

Constructed in 1997, this trail links Alder Lake with Balsam Lake Mountain, providing an ambitious day hike over Mill Brook

Ridge. A new lean-to midway along the route offers an enjoyable overnight experience as well.

▶ Trailhead: From Beaver Kill Road (see preceding description), drive eastward, turning left (north) on County Rt. 54 at Turnwood (0.0 mi). (This point is 3.5 mi east of the junction of Beaver Kill Road and Beech Hill Road.) Drive 2.6 mi north to the end of County Rt. 54 at the entrance to the Cross Mountain Camp (Old Edwards Road). Bear right to an immediate second junction, then bear right again on a gravel road. Drive until the road terminates at a barrier at 3.0 mi. The Alder Lake Trail parking lot is on the left. ◀

Beyond the barrier gate are a sign and trail register. Follow the roadway past the barrier a short distance to the remains of the old Coykendall Lodge. Turn right and follow a path down a grade to the shore of Alder Lake, a dam, and a DEC signpost at 0.1 mi.

From the DEC signpost, turn north (away from the dam) and follow the shoreline path around the north side of Alder Lake. At just under 0.2 mi, the first of three well-spaced designated campsite side trails is reached. Soon after, red trail markers are seen; these should be followed on this part of the trail. The attractive trail continues past some high bushes to another designated campsite at 0.6 mi before crossing a bridge shortly after. A second bridge is crossed 200 ft farther along the trail, then the route edges away from the lake and gradually climbs.

The trail bears left at a narrow fork at 0.7 mi, and 20 ft farther bears right onto a broad woods road. The woods road gradually ascends a grade and bears right again at each of two forks. The second fork is at the top of the knoll, where the trail reaches a junction with the trail ascending Mill Brook Ridge at 0.8 mi. Follow the yellow foot-trail markers east up a short grade along an old woods road.

At 1.0 mi the trail crests a hill and briefly descends before resuming its gradual ascent at 1.1 mi. The trail crosses a small stream at 1.2 mi and then passes through an old log landing. At 1.3 mi the trail begins a short, steep climb after which the grade moderates. A herd path forks right at 1.7 mi, leading to the first of three beaver meadows that the trail passes.

The woods road the trail has been following ends at a stream crossing at 1.8 mi; the hiking trail turns left and continues as a footpath.

At 1.9 mi another stream is crossed by way of a single log hewed flat. The trail turns left at 2.0 mi and begins a moderate ascent, following a brook to the right. At 2.1 mi the grade eases. The brook is now at the bottom of a steep ravine on the right.

At 2.2 mi the trail turns left as it reaches a second beaver meadow.

The trail skirts around the north side of the meadow and reaches a junction with two paths at 2.3 mi. The path on the right leads 80 ft to a lean-to overlooking the beaver meadow. The path to the left leads 100 ft to a pipe spring. The lean-to is 2.3 mi east of the Alder Lake trailhead and 4.5 mi west of Balsam Lake Mountain.

After leaving the lean-to, the trail turns north, climbing to a beaver pond and crossing its outlet on large rocks at 2.4 mi. After crossing a seasonal watercourse, the trail begins to climb moderately, following a drainage up Mill Brook Ridge. After a rather steep ascent near the top of the drainage, the trail reaches the top of the ridge at 2.9 mi and turns east. It soon passes a rock ledge on the left and swings east-southeast, passing a modest vista at 3.3 mi.

At 3.4 mi the trail climbs steeply with a switchback before reaching a vista to the west at 3.6 mi. Just beyond the vista, the trail crosses over the highest point on the ridge (3480 ft) and then begins a moderate descent as it follows the ridge east.

At 4.0 mi the trail levels. It swings south and passes the first view (through the trees) of Beecher Lake at 4.3 mi. The trail climbs gradually, turning sharply left at 4.4 mi and passing through a rocky ledge before switching back south. At 4.8 mi the trail reaches the top of a large rock ledge with a wonderful view of Beecher Lake and the Beaver Kill Range to the south.

Leaving the vista, the trail turns back east, easily climbs over another high point on the ridge (3420 ft) at 4.9 mi and then gradually descends, crossing a very small seasonal drainage at 5.2 mi. Continuing east on a nearly level traverse, the trail reaches a view of Balsam Lake Mountain, including the fire tower, at 5.4 mi.

Turning sharply north, the trail begins a steep descent to the col between Mill Brook Ridge and Balsam Lake Mountain. At 5.5 mi the grade moderates as the trail swings gradually east.

Reaching the col at 5.6 mi, the trail turns east-southeast, climbing gradually until reaching a short but steep ascent at 5.8 mi. After turning sharply right and ascending a ledge, the trail turns east and follows along the top of the ledge, a sort of shelf from which one gets good views of a mature hardwood forest. The trail turns south and passes a vista of a pair of beaver ponds in the Balsam Lake drainage at 6.0 mi.

Continuing south along the shelf, the trail crosses a seasonal spring at 6.1 mi, after which it begins a moderate ascent of Balsam Lake Mountain. After a few switchbacks and occasional steep climbs, the trail reaches a junction with a path to the most scenic vista on the mountain at 6.5 mi. Straight (north) 50 ft is the view of the western Catskills from a fern glade.

The trail turns sharply right and heads east over level ground to join the red-marked Balsam Lake Mountain Trail at 6.6 mi. (See above.) Turn left to reach the summit of Balsam Lake Mountain at 6.7 mi. A spring is beside the trail 0.35 mi south; the Balsam Lake Mountain lean-to is 0.4 mi south; and the Balsam Lake Mountain trailhead parking lot at the end of Beaver Kill Road is 1.7 mi south.

Hunter Mountain

The original fire tower on Hunter Mountain was constructed in 1909, one of the first of three towers built in the Catskills that year. This wooden tower was 40 ft tall and was replaced by a steel tower in 1917. The steel tower was moved from its original location 0.2 mi northward to its present site in 1953. It has the distinction of being located on the highest point, 4040 ft, of any such tower in New York State.

Like other Forest Preserve fire towers, the Hunter tower was abandoned as an active fire detection site in 1990, and by the mid-nineties was condemned by the DEC for public use. In 1998, signs of rejuvenation appeared at the tower, thanks to the work of DEC personnel and the Hunter Mountain Fire Tower Committee. In 1999, the tower's steps, landings, and the floor of the cab were replaced, the roof was replaced, and the steel given a fresh coat of paint. New cab windows were installed in spring 2000 and the tower was reopened in October of that year. For more information and to find out how you can help with the tower's continued maintenance, see Appendix A.

The fire tower on Hunter's summit can be reached by hiking from three different trailheads over (1) the Becker Hollow and Becker Hollow Connector Trails from the northeast, (2) the Devil's Path and Hunter Mountain Spur Trail from the southeast, and (3) the Spruceton Trail from the northwest. The author hesitates to mention a fourth route, which some may consider of dubious outdoor ethics, namely the ski lift ride from the Hunter Ski Bowl on the north side of the mountain to the Colonel's Chair. From here via the yellow Colonel's Chair Trail and the last section of the Spruceton Trail one still has a 2.1-mile walk and a 940-ft vertical ascent to the tower. Your choice. We describe all four routes.

The trail summary information that precedes each of the following descriptions assumes that the hiker is retracing his or her steps. Many hikers also enjoy climbing this mountain by one route and descending to a car left in advance at a different trailhead. For instance, one may leave a car at the Devil's Path trailhead for a descent and ascend the Becker Hollow Trail. These two trailheads are only 1.6 mi apart along NY 214, a distance easily walked should you have only one vehicle.

Becker Hollow Trail

Round-trip Distance: 4.4 mi (7.0 km) via Connector Trail, or 4.6 mi (7.4 km) via 0.2 mi of Spruceton Trail
Elevation Change: 2210 ft (674 m)
Summit Elevation: 4040 ft (1231 m)
Difficulty: (3) A challenging route, relentlessly steep in upper reaches.
Maps: NE Catskill Map 41 (M-4) or Hunter 7.5'

This is the shortest trail to the summit of Hunter Mountain. It ascends 2200 ft at a steady grade, a rather tough climb. Of interest to forest observers is the dramatic passage from logged-over second growth to a section of old-growth forest at the 3060-ft contour. Though it is not marked with signage, the careful observer will note

a distinct transition from trees of modest diameter to giant sugar maples and yellow birch, among other large species.

▶ Trailhead: Trail access is on the west side of NY 214 at the DEC trail sign and parking area 1.3 mi south of NY 23A. A trail register is at the trailhead. ◀

The trail heads west on a gravel roadway, past a vehicle barrier, following blue DEC trail markers.

Observer's cabin viewed from the Hunter Mountain tower (1997). DEC and the Hunter Fire Tower Committee have since restored the cabin.

Brian Sullivan

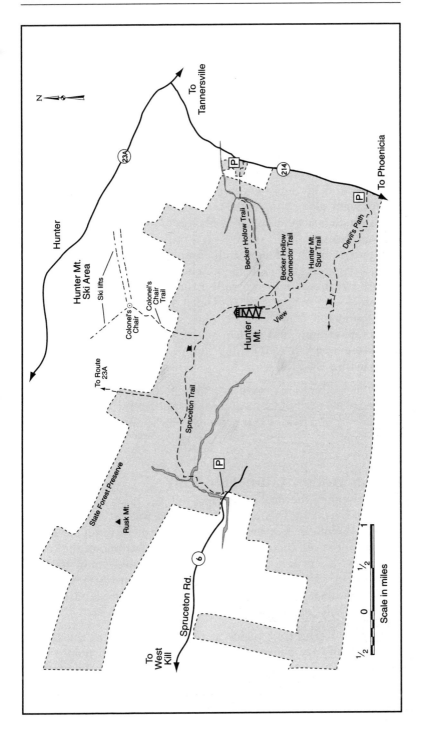

At 0.1 mi the route enters hardwood forest. Shortly after, the gravel trail branches left, while the hiking trail continues straight ahead. It soon parallels a brook, which it crosses on a footbridge at 0.3 mi. (Avoid the unmarked path to the right.)

At 0.4 mi, the trail passes a three-tiered cascade of the brook and then a 50-ft concrete dam. Once across a creek at 0.5 mi, a pitch up pulls away from the water. The way is still wide as the old woods road ascends the mountain. The grade eases briefly at 0.9 mi before resuming its moderate slope. A sign indicating an elevation of 3500 ft is reached at 1.8 mi. A fieldstone path guides hikers through an open area to a junction at 1.9 mi. (A spring is 250 ft to the right along the yellow-marked Becker Hollow Connector Trail, which leads 0.3 mi to the fire tower on the Hunter Mt. summit; see below).

The blue Becker Hollow Trail continues straight ahead up several steep pitches to a four-way junction at 2.1 mi. Steel rods at the former fire tower site protrude from the bedrock. The yellow Hunter Mountain Spur Trail goes left 1.4 mi to the Devil's Path, the blue Spruceton Trail to the right leads 0.2 mi to the fire tower on the actual summit, and straight ahead, a short level path westward brings one to a ledge with a fine view of southwest Hunter and the valley of the West Kill.

Trail in winter: This route is a fine snowshoe route, but a real challenge on skis. Skiers will find the Spruceton Trail, which follows an old jeep road, a better choice. See Spruceton Trail description below.

Becker Hollow Connector Trail

When climbing the Becker Hollow Trail, the hiker can save a few minutes by taking this connector on the way to the summit of Hunter Mountain. A spring provides a source of water for hikers who need to refill their water bottles. The condition of the trail is less stable than that of other trails on the mountain, but it is pleasant to walk. The route leads past what forestry professor Michael Kudish believes is the highest elevation stand of sugar maples in the Catskills.

▶ Trailhead: The trail begins at the 1.9-mi point of the Becker Hollow Trail (see above) and climbs to the 3.4 mi point of the Spruceton Trail (see below), at the summit of Hunter Mountain. ◀

From the junction at the 1.9 mi point of the Becker Hollow Trail, the yellow-marked trail very gradually descends northwest 250 ft through a wet area to good spring water delivered from a metal pipe. The trail then travels on contour 0.2 mi, where it swings left and pitches upward through conifers. One has to be careful to follow trail markers here. It enters the northwest edge of the clearing at the summit of Hunter Mountain at 0.3 mi adjacent to the fire tower.

Devil's Path and Hunter Mountain Spur Trail

Round-trip Distance: 7.5 mi (12.1 km) via Spur Trail and
0.2 mi of Spruceton Trail
Elevation Change: 2060 ft (628 m)
Summit Elevation: 4040 ft (1231 m)
Difficulty: (4) Rugged trail, quite steep.
Maps: NE Catskill Map 41 (M-4) or Hunter 7.5'

This is the heart of the Devil's territory in the Catskills and has some extremely steep climbing. It is not a place in which to rush, for you may have a devil of a time.

The original fire tower on Hunter Mountain was located where the Becker Hollow Trail now ends, near the summit of Hunter. The Hunter Mountain Spur Trail and the Spruceton Trail also ended at this spot. When the present tower was moved to the actual summit in 1953, the trails were not rerouted to end at the new tower site. Consequently, the trail markers are the same as originally set out, and the Hunter Mountain Spur and Spruceton Trails still both end at the original tower site. This is why hikers sometimes become confused when the trail markers they have been following up the Hunter Mountain Spur or Becker Hollow Trails suddenly change color 0.2 mi before the true summit is reached.

▶ Trailhead: The trailhead and parking area are on the west side of NY 214, 2.9 mi south of the junction of NY 214 and NY 23A, east of the village of Hunter. At this trailhead the Devil's Path drops off Plateau Mountain and then climbs the flanks of Hunter Mountain. ◀

The route passes through the parking area on the west side of the road. Leaving the left rear of the parking area, it bears right, following red DEC trail markers.

After 100 ft the trail drops down a bank and crosses the outlet of Notch Lake on a wide log bridge below a small cement dam. It then heads southwest, reaching a trail register at 0.1 mi. From there, the trail continues to the base of a rock bluff at 0.3 mi, where large boulders seem to surround you. Continue straight ahead up the sloping rock.

The grade steepens, with some excellent stone trail work, to a second rock bluff at 0.35 mi. After following the base of the cliff, the trail climbs very steeply up a 50-ft vertical zone known as the Devil's Portal, passing a small stone overhang before reaching the top of the wall.

(Years ago, another trail left the main trail at the top of the Devil's Portal and led to the Devil's Pulpit, above the stone face of the Devil, at the cliffs to the north. It is nearly impossible to locate this path today.)

The trail continues to climb at varying steep, moderate, and gradual grades to 1.8 mi, where it levels and contours a side slope, having ascended 1500 ft from Stony Clove Notch.

The trail reaches the Hunter Mt. Spur Trail junction at 2.15 mi at a 3500 ft elevation. The Hunter Mountain summit can be reached in another 1.6 mi from this junction via the yellow Hunter Mountain Spur Trail and a 0.2 mi section of the blue Spruceton Trail.

The Hunter Mountain Spur Trail leaves its junction with the Devil's Path and very gradually ascends Hunter Mountain to the northeast following yellow trail markers. It begins a counterclockwise swing to the northwest at 0.3 mi, following a wide old woods road. At 1.0 mi the trail steepens briefly as it climbs two switchbacks. It then resumes its nearly flat grade to the junction with the Becker Hollow Trail to the right at 1.4 mi. This four-way junction is the original site of the fire tower, now relocated 0.2 mi straight ahead along the blue-blazed Spruceton Trail. At this point a short level walk to the left (west) brings one to ledges with a good view of southwest Hunter and the valley of the West Kill.

Trail in winter: Too steep for skis, but this trail lends itself to snowshoes with crampons.

Spruceton Trail

Round-trip Distance:	6.8 mi (10.9 km)
Elevation Change:	1,950 ft (594 m)
Summit Elevation:	4040 ft (1231 m)
Difficulty:	(2) A well-graded, moderately steep route along an old jeep road.
Maps:	NE Catskill Map 41 (L-4, 3 to M-4) or Lexington 7.5' and Hunter 7.5'

The Spruceton Trail follows the Hunter Mountain fire tower jeep road from the end of the Spruceton Road all the way to the summit of Hunter Mountain. Relatively easy to climb, this route is attractive and enjoyable to hike.

▶ Trailhead: Beginning at the hamlet of West Kill on NY 42, proceed east along the Spruceton Road (County Rt. 6), passing two DEC parking areas on the right (south) side at 2.9 and 3.8 mi, to a very large DEC parking area and the trailhead on the left (north) side at 6.7 mi. ◀

The level trail with DEC blue trail markers leaves the northeast end of the parking area. A yellow barrier gate blocks vehicles, and the route soon parallels the east side of Hunter Brook, reaching a trail register at 0.3 mi.

The trail turns left at an open campsite on the right at 0.4 mi, and crosses Hunter Brook on a wide bridge. A steady moderate upgrade reaches a sharp switchback at 0.5 mi. (This is the starting point for the climb of Rusk Mountain.) Occasional switchbacks and steady grades end at a height of land at 1.7 mi, where the trail turns right. (Avoid continuing straight ahead on the old Hunter Road down through Taylor Hollow towards Deming Road.)

The trail now becomes a twisting moderate grade. A yellow-marked spur trail right, with a log fence, at 2.2 mi leads 100 ft to an open area with a stone fireplace. Beyond the fireplace 200 ft is a good spring, with water gushing from a metal pipe. This is a very pleasant camping spot.

Gradual grades continue to the site of the former John Robb lean-to, left of the trail at 2.3 mi. This lean-to burned down in 2005. There are good views west and northwest across the trail from the lean-to site.

At a junction at 2.4 mi the yellow-marked Colonel's Chair Trail heads left (north) 1.1 mi to a ski lodge and chairlift, at the Colonel's Chair. (This is a good emergency escape route. See reverse trail description, below.)

The trail essentially levels at 2.5 mi, with only an occasional short upgrade. A brook runoff at 2.9 mi leads 40 ft to the top of an old glacial meltoff waterfall. Almost dry now, it shows evidence of once having had more water.

The Spruceton Trail climbs a moderate grade at 3.3 mi, reaching the western edge of the very large summit clearing for the restored (2000) Hunter Mountain fire tower and observer's cabin at 3.4 mi. It is necessary to climb the fire tower for a view; for those who do, a 360-degree panorama awaits. The Blackhead Range is to the northeast, Kaaterskill High Peak can be seen to the east, the Devil's

Path mountains are to the south, West Kill Mountain is to the west.

The Becker Hollow Connector Trail (see above) leaves the northwest edge of the clearing.

The Spruceton Trail was designed to end at the original fire tower site south of the present location. It continues from the summit clearing to the southeast along the flat ridge and ends at 3.6 mi where the original fire tower stood at a four-way junction of the blue Becker Hollow Trail, to the left, and the yellow Hunter Mountain Spur Trail, ahead. Because it is well above 3500 ft. elevation, the former Hunter Mountain lean-to has been removed, and the scattered open sites around this junction are no longer used for camping. This is necessary to protect the fragile summit vegetation from destruction. To the right at this junction is a short level trail to ledges with a splendid view of southwest Hunter and the valley of the West Kill.

Trail in winter: All but perhaps 0.3 mi is skiable but suitable for expert skiers only. Skiers may want to carry snowshoes for this short section.

Colonel's Chair Trail

Round-trip Distance
  (via Spruceton Trail): 4.2 mi (6.7 km)
Elevation Change
  (on foot):   940 ft (287 m)
Summit Elevation: 4040 ft (1231 m)
Difficulty: (2) The shortest and easiest approach
                          to Hunter Mt., easy in comparison to
                          the other three options; but still 2.1 mi
                          of uphill walking.
Maps: NE Catskill Map 41 (M-3) or Hunter 7.5'

This Hunter Mountain route is unique in that one must first take a chairlift at the Hunter Mountain Ski Bowl up the ski slope to a lodge atop the Colonel's Chair, a knob on the northern shoulder of the mountain. This spot was named for Colonel William Edwards, a leather tanner in this region in the early 1800s. From the valley floor, this bump on Hunter's shoulder resembles a chair.

Both summer hikers and winter snowshoe climbers can ride the chairlift and then continue on to the summit of Hunter Mountain. The chairlift normally operates until 4:30 each day, though the hiker had best verify this before starting out, especially if inclement weather is predicted.

▶ Trailhead: The trail leaves the upper-level exit of the lodge and heads generally south, following yellow DEC trail markers. ◀

The route passes a group of picnic tables, charcoal burners, and the starting points for several downhill ski runs. At 0.1 mi there is a monument commemorating John Clair, for his contributions to skiing, and Jean Wald, who lost his life while serving as a member of the ski patrol. Follow a grassy path left of the service road a short distance before rejoining it. Avoid the windmills and other apparatus on the right side of the trail at 0.2 mi. Continue along the flat trail to a junction at 0.5 mi. Then bear left and begin gradual climbing past the 3500 ft elevation level at 1.0 mi. The moderate grade levels just before the trail reaches a junction with the Spruceton Trail at 1.1 mi.

By turning left and walking another 1.0 mi up the Spruceton Trail, the hiker can reach the fire tower summit of 4040-ft. Hunter Mountain, the second highest peak in the Catskills.

Trail in winter: Snowshoes recommended; too difficult for most skiers.

Overlook Mountain

Round-trip Distance: 5.0 mi (8 km)
Elevation Change: 1400 ft (427 m)
Summit Elevation: 3140 ft (957 m)
Difficulty: (2) A moderate hike along a gravel road, never very steep.
Maps: NE Catskill Map 41 (0-5) or Woodstock 7.5'

Far above the Hudson Valley near Woodstock is Overlook Mountain, with its newly restored fire tower, the first of the five Catskill towers to be officially reopened for safe public use. A rededication ceremony at the tower on June 5, 1999, allowed volunteers of the Overlook Fire Tower Committee to show off the tower's spectacular 360-degree view to DEC officials, specially invited guests, and the general public.

The Overlook fire tower is the newest of the five remaining towers in the Catskills. Originally built in 1927, it stood on Gallis Hill west of Kingston, New York, until 1950 when it was moved to its present location. It was abandoned by DEC for fire observing in 1989 and was subsequently closed to the public. Ten years later, successful restoration has made its breathtaking views again

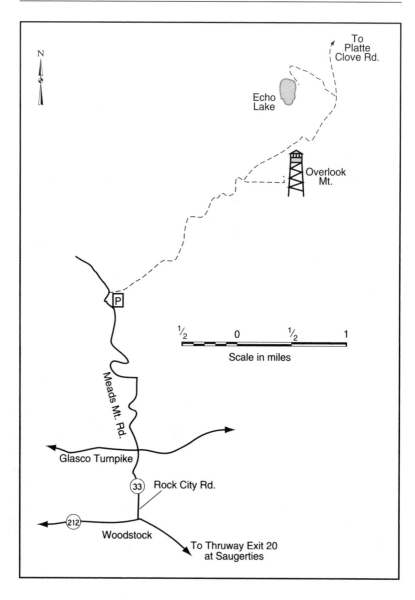

available to hikers. The job of its continued maintenance and additional enhancements will occupy area citizens well into the new century. For more information and to contribute to these efforts, see Appendix A.

The trail to Overlook's summit follows the unusually gradual grade of an old carriage road. Pierre DeLabigarre, a French Revolutionist, was probably the first to write about the views from this mountain, after his climb in 1793. In 1833 James Booth built a "temporary" hotel there. It took until 1871 to establish a permanent hotel. It burned to the ground on April Fools' Day in 1874, when no one would believe a small child who tried to convince staff that the smoke in the chimney was darker than usual. Rebuilt in 1878, it burned down again in 1924. The struggle to keep it open ended in 1939, in the midst of rebuilding yet again. Remnants of the half-finished foundations are still visible.

▶ Trailhead: Access to the Overlook Mountain trailhead is from Woodstock. From the Village Green travel 0.6 mi north on County Rt. 33 (Rock City Road) to its intersection with Glasco Turnpike. Continue 2.1 mi straight ahead up steep Meads Mountain Road to the DEC trailhead signpost and large parking area on the right side of the road. The large building across the road from the trailhead was once Mead's Mountain House, an early hotel. ◀

The trail runs east from the trail register on a wide gravel road. Red DEC trail markers guide you but are not needed. The gradual upgrade is steady, with broad switchbacks all the way to the junction with the Old Overlook Road Trail.

There is a pipe with gushing water on the left side of the road at 0.35 mi. A less obvious spring is on the side of the road at 0.5 mi. Large boulders along the way show signs of frequent use as resting spots, but the way is so easy that a side trip to Echo Lake (see below) is almost necessary to make a full day's outing.

At 1.1 mi there is a fork; bear left. The ruins of the Overlook Mt. House are on the right at 1.8 mi. The trail circles around to

Overlook Mountain tower, restored to public use. At its rededication, June 1999.

the rear of the ruins, passing a large antenna, several smaller buildings, and an old stone foundation. It reaches a junction with the
Old Overlook Road at 2.0 mi. (The Old Overlook Road Trail with
blue DEC markers branches left 2.0 mi to Echo Lake and 4.8 mi to
Platte Clove Road.)

Straight ahead, the Overlook Mountain Trail is now almost level.
There is a yellow barrier gate at 2.1 mi. The trail heads east where
a path leads to a viewing point on the right at 2.2 mi. The trail
gradually climbs, circling below the summit, to the fire observer's
cabin at 2.5 mi. A fireplace and picnic table are across the road
from the cabin. Views are best from the fire tower, which provides
magnificent vistas in all directions. The Hudson stands out in the
east; Ashokan Reservoir is to the south; Slide, Cornell, and
Wittenberg Mountains are to the west; Indian Head, Twin, Sugarloaf,
Plateau, and Hunter Mountains are to the north.

Trail in winter: Both the Overlook Mountain Trail and the Old Overlook Road Trail make fine skiing and snowshoeing routes.

Red Hill

Round-trip Distance: 2.8 mi (4.5 km)
Elevation Change: 890 ft (297 m)
Summit Elevation: 2990 ft (911 m)
Difficulty: (1) A short hike, never very steep.
Maps: Claryville 7.5'

Red Hill in southern Ulster County was selected in 1920 as the
southernmost Catskill site for a steel fire lookout station, bypassing
the slightly higher Denman Mountain nearby. It was the last staffed
tower in the Catskill Forest Preserve, the post of a DEC observer
until 1990. From the late 1930s till the mid-seventies, observers,
along with the general public, used an access road from the south.
When the private land over which it ran was sold, the new owner
denied access. No official easement had ever been obtained by the
state for this road, so access today is over state Forest Preserve
land by way of a new yellow-blazed foot trail from the north built
by members of the New York–New Jersey Trail Conference and DEC
in 1996.

A slice of Forest Preserve land, an isolated piece of the Sundown
Wild Forest in the Town of Denning, encompasses the summit of

Red Hill and borders on Coons (formerly Dinch) Road. In 2001, DEC built a five-car parking lot at the trailhead. Adirondack hikers will be interested to learn that DEC Forest Rangers Pete Fish and Steve Ovitt served the Red Hill area before transfer to the Adirondacks.

A volunteer group of local citizens under the leadership of Helen and George Elias has renovated Red Hill's tower in cooperation with DEC, the Catskill Center for Conservation and Development, and skilled volunteers from a local iron works. In 1999, new steel cross braces, bolts, and new roofing for the observer's cabin were flown to the summit by helicopter. The group reopened the tower in Summer 2000 and has restored the observer's cabin. Volunteers keep the tower cab open during summer and fall weekends. For more information and to contribute to the effort, see Appendix A.

▶ Trailhead: From the north, take Kingston Exit 19 of the NYS Thruway, following Rt. 28 signs to the west; then turn south on NY 209 toward Ellenville. Proceed southwest 26 miles on NY 209, then turn right (west) on NY 55. After 6 miles, keep right on 55A. Continue another 7 mi, passing north of Rondout Reservoir and dam, to a T intersection. Turn right on County Rt. 153 (Peekamoose Road) towards Sundown and Shokan. After 0.2 mi, turn left on Sugar Loaf Road. Continue uphill 4.2 mi, making an abrupt left turn on Red Hill Road. After 100 yds Coons Road goes right; a gravel lot on the left makes a convenient meeting spot. Reset your trip odometer to 0.0 here. Drive up unpaved Coons Road past a height of land and the unmarked Rudolph Road to the right at 0.6 mi. (Beyond this point, road is not maintained in winter.) Continue downhill along Coons Road despite a "Dead End" sign. Avoid a left turn into a private driveway at 0.7 mi. At 0.9 mi a wide spot on the right provides turn-in parking for 3–4 cars. The trailhead and 5-car parking lot are farther downhill on the left at 1.2 mi.

From the south, the intersection of NY 209 and NY 55 can be reached from NY 17 by driving 15 mi north along NY 209 through Ellenville.

From the west, leave NY 17 at Liberty, following NY 55 east to a junction with Rt. 55A just past Grahamsville, then left (north) on 55A to a junction with County Rt. 153 (Peekamoose Road), and straight ahead on Rt. 153 to Sugar Loaf Road. Follow directions given above. ◀

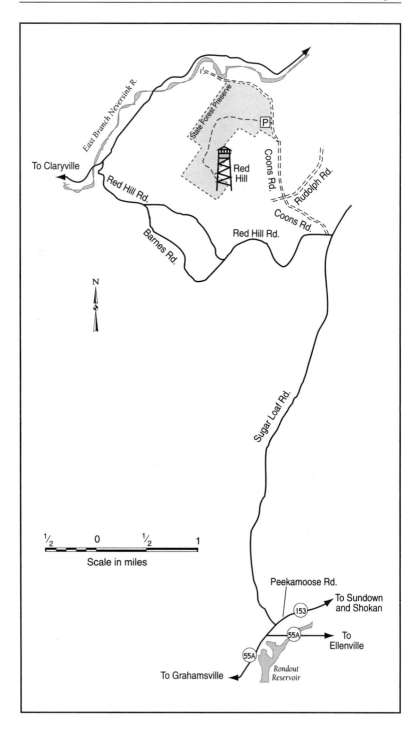

Leaving Dinch Road, the trail traverses attractive, mature, second growth hardwoods of maple, beech, cherry, poplar, and ash. Watch carefully for yellow DEC trail markers in the first half of the route where the footway is still ill defined. At 0.1 mi, cross an often-dry creek bed and begin a steeper ascent. At 0.2 mi, the trail angles up to the right with exposed bedrock ledges on the left and passes a small hemlock grove at 0.5 mi on the right.

At 0.7 mi, bear right where the trail merges with an old wagon road coming in from the left. Along this section, rock piles and uniform tree size on the right indicate an old farm. Leave the wagon road at 0.8 mi, following yellow markers to the left more steeply uphill. The trail alternates between uphill and level sections for the next half-mile until, at 1.3 mi, it levels off for the last time and the fire tower can be glimpsed between the trees ahead. The observer's cabin is passed on the right and a smaller utility building and outhouse on the left. The 60-foot tower is reached at 1.4 mi in a pleasant clearing surrounded by large maple and red spruce, the latter thought to have been planted.

Views from the tower, the most southerly such outpost in the Catskill Park, are impressive. To the south, the three bodies of water are all sections of the Rondout Reservoir, part of the complex New York City water supply system. Water flows here from reservoirs on the East and West Branches of the Delaware River and from the Neversink drainage through underground aqueducts. Above Rondout Reservoir, the Shawangunk ridge is on the horizon. Looking far leftward to the southeast, with small binoculars one can pick out Mohonk's Sky Top Tower. To the east, right to left, one sees Peekamoose, Table, and Lone Mountains. Left of Lone Mountain are Balsam Cap and Friday Mountains in the distance. The next peak left and the apparent highest is Slide Mountain, which is indeed the highest point in the Catskills. Looking north, there are three summits. The rightmost one with a distinctive flat top is Doubletop Mountain. In the middle is Graham Mountain, and to its left Balsam Lake Mountain, whose summit fire tower is visible with low-power binoculars or even the keen naked eye on a clear day. To the southwest the horizon is dominated by the nearby and slightly higher Denman Mountain, at 3053 ft. Our perch in Red Hill's tower, however, brings us to its height.

Trail in winter: The route to the trailhead, especially the last 1.2 mi along Dinch Road, is not plowed in winter. But having walked or skied to the trailhead, the climber may well prefer snowshoes to skis. The first half of the route is narrow and not well-defined enough to recommend for skiing.

Mount Tremper

At one time, this centrally located peak was one of the most frequently climbed in the Catskills, owing to its modest hiking distance and the superb view from the tower. The fire tower was built about 1917 and was used for fire detection until 1975. By the 1990s it had deteriorated, and conditions were not safe for ascent. In June 1999, however, the local Mount Tremper Fire Tower Restoration Project, under DEC auspices and $3000 in funding, with assistance from members of the national Forest Fire Lookout Association, began the work of replacing the stairs, landings, and floor of the upper cab. Additional renovations proceeded in 2000. The tower's formal reopening occurred on June 9, 2001, under blue skies and with superlative views from the cab. For restoration information and to contribute to this project, see Appendix A.

Originally named Timothy Berg, the mountain was renamed for Major Jacob H. Tremper of Kingston, who, with Captain William C. Romer, owned the Tremper House. This large hotel was one of the first to offer visitors to the Catskills an opportunity to arrive at its door by railroad, with no bumpy stagecoaches needed for transport.

Rattlesnakes are occasionally seen on this mountain, especially at the old quarry, where they enjoy sunning themselves on the broad rock faces.

Mount Tremper via the Willow Trail

Round-trip Distance: 6.4 mi (10.2 km)
Elevation Change: 1430 ft (437 m)
Summit Elevation: 2740 ft (838 m)
Difficulty: (2) A longish route with moderate grades.
Maps: NE Catskill Map 41 (M,L-5)
                          or Phoenicia 7.5'

The Willow Trail is the longer of the two trails to the Mount Tremper summit but saves 600 ft in elevation gain. While the Phoenicia Trail (below) is a short, steep climb, the Willow Trail ascends Hoyt Hollow through forest that becomes increasingly more attractive as you climb. If two vehicles are available, a through-trip ascending the Phoenicia Trail and descending the Willow Trail makes a very pleasant day's outing.

▶ Trailhead: Access is off NY 212 in the hamlet of Willow. Turn west onto Van Wagner Road and drive 0.4 mi to Jessup Road. Turn

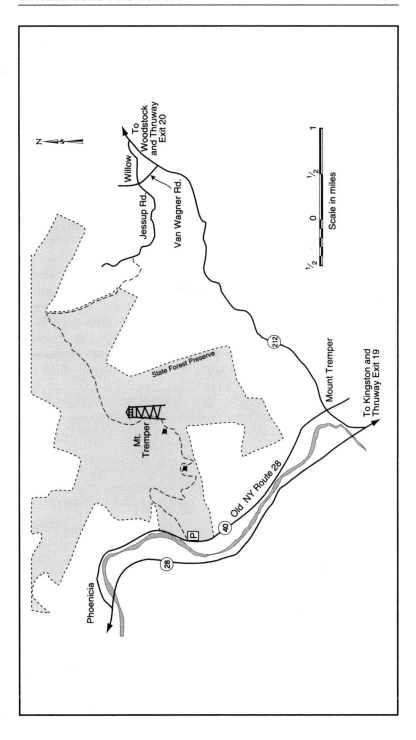

left and drive 1.0 mi on Jessup Road to the point where it begins to climb. This is the trailhead. There is no parking area; hikers need to ask landowners for permission to park on their property. ◀

Where Jessup Road begins to climb (0.0 mi.), the trail becomes a rough woods road. Blue DEC trail markers guide you. Avoid all side roads on the lower slopes.

From 0.2 to 0.5 mi, mountain laurel grows profusely. In late spring, their white and pink blooms literally form a wall on each side of the trail.

Yellow paint blazes mark the beginning of state land at 0.6 mi. The change in forest quality is very noticeable. At 0.9 mi the trail becomes a moderate grade. The wall of the hollow drops sharply off on the right, and the character of the forest becomes more primitive. The route turns left at 1.4 mi, steeply climbing to a ridgeline, which it reaches at 1.5 mi.

The route is now a well-marked wilderness path leading southwest. It gains elevation gradually and then levels. Views to the east occasionally present themselves through the trees. The pathway gradually gains elevation again at 2.6 mi and continues to do so all the way to the summit and fire tower at 3.2 mi. Ground level views are minimal; however, with renewed access to the tower, one can see Panther, Slide, and Wittenberg Mountains; Giant Ledges; the Ashokan Reservoir; and much more.

The red-marked Phoenicia Trail (see below) continues south and west, reaching the new parking lot on County Rt. 40 in another 3.1 mi. The Mount Tremper lean-to is just 0.05 mi from the tower along this trail.

Trail in winter: Snowshoers can use either the Phoenicia or Willow Trail, but parking is a problem at the Willow trailhead (see trailhead description). Skiers prefer the Phoenicia Trail, which follows an old jeep road.

Mount Tremper via the Phoenicia Trail

Round-trip Distance: 6.2 mi (9.9 km)
Elevation Change: 2030 ft (621 m)
Summit Elevation: 2740 ft (838 m)
Difficulty: (2) a moderate ascent along an old jeep road.
Maps: NE Catskill Map 41 (L-5) or Phoenicia 7.5'

The Phoenicia Trail is the shorter of the two trails to the Mount Tremper summit, but requires a 600-ft greater vertical ascent.

Brian Sullivan

Lean-to atop Mount Tremper (1999), scheduled for relocation

▶ Trailhead: The trailhead and DEC parking lot are on the north side of County Rt. 40 (old NY 28), 1.8 mi southeast of Phoenicia and 2.1 mi northwest of the settlement of Mount Tremper. The parking lot with about a 10-car capacity was built here by DEC in 1998. The trailhead was moved from its previous location to a spot 0.3 mi southeast on County Rt. 40 to accommodate hikers at the new lot. ◀

The red-marked trail leaves the northern end of the new parking lot, climbing parallel to the highway for a few hundred yards, then turning right (eastward) up rock steps. It proceeds over a knoll and down to a junction with the old jeep road at 0.4 mi where there is a DEC trail register. Turn uphill to the right. This old jeep road becomes less steep at 0.8 mi, swinging southeast and then south. The route levels again at 1.2 mi, where there is a spring on the left. The trail begins a series of switchbacks, passing a small waterfall on the right at 2.1 mi. Just after a sharp switchback at 2.2 mi, a spur trail right leads 100 ft. to the Baldwin Memorial lean-to.

The trail continues uphill to 2.3 mi, where a side trail left runs 30 ft. to a large boulder where water from a spring rushes out from a long metal pipe. At 2.8 mi the route levels, swinging northeast on a grassy lane. The Mount Tremper lean-to is on the left side of the trail at 3.0 mi.

The summit, marked by the fire tower, is reached at 3.1 mi.

The Fire Tower
Challenge

The Fire Tower Challenge

Whether it's the view from the summit or the tower—or the experiences enroute—"fire tower fever" grips you right away and there's no turning back. Sound familiar? Then you're a person for whom ADK's Glens Falls–Saratoga Chapter has created the Fire Tower Challenge.

Consider the spectacular views of the surrounding hills and valleys, the wildlife you may see along the way, and the botanically interesting summit vegetation. And consider that for some 50–70 years the cabs atop these towers were the outlooks of "fire spotters," observers whose lonesome vigil was broken only occasionally by visits from the public.

You don't need to be a member of ADK to take part in the Fire Tower Challenge. If you do wish to join, ADK chapters plan a wide variety of activities to help you learn more about nature, outdoor skills, and the protection of our environment. Chapter outings schedules can even help you achieve your Challenge goals. For more information, call 1-800-395-8080 (8:30 AM–5:00 PM, Mon.–Sat.), visit on-line at <www.adk.org>, or visit our Lake George and Heart Lake facilities.

Rules of the Challenge

1. The Challenge began with the publication of this guidebook.
2. To complete the Challenge and receive the official full-color patch, hikers must climb and document, by date, ascents of at least 23 fire tower summits: 18 of 23 Adirondack Park summits and all 5 Catskill Park summits. *Climbing each tower itself is not required, nor in fact recommended, for those towers that have not been restored for safe public use.*
3. The mountain should have a standing fire tower on the date of your ascent. Several of the Adirondack towers described in this guide may eventually be removed. (See below, Adirondack Park Fire Towers That May Not Last.) You may want to check their status with the DEC (see Appendix A) before you climb.
4. When registering the dates of your hikes below, be sure to use extra sheets of paper to describe details of interest: weather, wildlife sightings, your impressions, your companions—and whatever else caught your attention. We really want you to share your experiences with us, so please be expressive.
5. Send a photocopy of the following checklist and additional pages—name and address on each—along with a check for $3.00 per patch. (Children 15 and under are free.) Make the check payable to "ADK Glens Falls–Saratoga Chapter" and send to:

Fire Tower Challenge
Glens Falls–Saratoga Chapter, Adirondack Mountain Club
P.O. Box 2314, Glens Falls, NY 12801

Your Personal Log

Name_____

Address_____

_____

SUMMITS WITH FIRE TOWERS

Adirondack Park Fire Towers with a Bright Future

Mount Arab .... ○   Date: _____

Azure Mountain .... ○   Date: _____

Bald (Rondaxe) Mountain .... ○   Date: _____

Belfry Mountain .... ○   Date: _____

Black Mountain............................... ○   Date: _____

Blue Mountain .... ○   Date: _____

Cathedral Rock .... ○   Date: _____

Goodnow Mountain .... ○   Date: _____

Gore Mountain................................ ○   Date: _____

Hadley Mountain .... ○   Date: _____

Kane Mountain .... ○   Date: _____

Owls Head Mountain .... ○   Date: _____

Pillsbury Mountain .... ○   Date: _____

Poke-O-Moonshine Mountain ..... ○   Date: _____

Snowy Mountain .... ○   Date: _____

Vanderwacker Mountain .... ○   Date: _____

Wakely Mountain .... ○   Date: _____

Woodhull Mountain .... ○   Date: _____

Adirondack Park Fire Towers That May Not Last

Mount Adams.................................. ○   Date: _____

Hurricane Mountain .... ○   Date: _____

Lyon Mountain .... ○   Date: _____

Spruce Mountain .... ○   Date: _____

St. Regis Mountain......................... ○   Date: _____

Catskill Park Fire Towers

Balsam Lake Mountain .... ○   Date: _____

Hunter Mountain .... ○   Date: _____

Overlook Mountain........................ ○   Date: _____

Red Hill .... ○   Date: _____

Mount Tremper.............................. ○   Date: _____

Sources and Resources

▶ *Fire Tower Restoration and Maintenance*

Looking to contribute dollars or work on a favorite fire tower project? Interested in spearheading a tower restoration project or helping with maintenance? The following references may prove helpful.

Mount Arab
Friends of Mount Arab (FOMA)
P.O. Box 185
Piercefield, N.Y. 12973
Or call FOMA chair Darwin (Tony) Gensel at 518-359-9146.

Azure Mountain
Azure Mountain Friends
c/o Carolyn Kaczka
P.O. Box 302
Hannawa Falls, NY 13647
315-265-4806

Balsam Lake Mountain
Friends of the Balsam Lake Fire Tower
c/o Rich Roller
18 Woodfield Rd.
Washington Township, NJ 07675
201-746-0018
ranger31@optonline.net

Blue Mountain
Greg George, Forest Ranger
NYS Department of Environmental Conservation
Rt. 28
Blue Mountain Lake, N.Y. 12812
518-352-7676

Cathedral Rock
Lawrence Rathman or Chris Westbrook
SUNY College of Environmental Science and Forestry Ranger School
P.O. Box 48
Wanakena, N.Y. 13695
315-848-2566

Goodnow Mountain
Adirondack Ecological Center, Attn: Ray Masters
6312 State Route 28N
Newcomb, NY 12852
518-582-4551

Hadley Mountain
Hadley Fire Tower Committee
c/o Jack Freeman, Committee Secretary
11 Arbor Drive
Glens Falls, N.Y. 12801
518-792-9659
or
Steven Guenther, Forest Ranger
NYS Department of Environmental Conservation
1424 Hadley Hill Road
Hadley, N.Y. 12835
518-696-2893

Hunter Mountain
Rick Dearstyne, Forest Ranger
NYS Department of Environmental Conservation
P.O. Box 8
West Kill, N.Y. 12492
518-989-6255

Kane Mountain
Canada Lakes Protective Association
c/o William Fielding
Canada Lake Store and Marina
Rts. 29A and 30
Caroga Lake, NY 12032
518-835-6069
Contributions may be made by check payable to the Association. Send to:
    Richard Fink, Treasurer
    Canada Lakes Protective Association
    1186 Wendel Avenue
    Schenectady, N.Y. 12308

Overlook Mountain
Overlook Fire Tower Stewards
c/o Dick Voloshen
34 Wardwell Lane
Woodstock, N.Y. 12498
845-679-2580
volo@ulster.net

Owls Head Mountain
Friends of Owls Head Fire Tower
c/o Ruth Howe
HCO1 Box 50, Deerland Road
Long Lake, NY 12847
518-624-2162
ruthhowe@frontiernet.net

Poke-O-Moonshine Mountain
Friends of Poke-O-Moonshine
c/o David Thomas-Train
P.O. Box 41
Keene Valley, N.Y. 12943
518-576-4592

Red Hill
Red Hill Fire Tower Committee
c/o Helen and George Elias
P.O. Box 24
Grahamsville, N.Y. 12740
845-985-7274 (May–Oct.) or 352-726-6695 (Nov.–April)

Snowy Mountain
Greg George, Forest Ranger
NYS Department of Environmental Conservation
Route 28
Blue Mountain Lake, N.Y. 12812
518-352-7676

Mount Tremper
Mount Tremper Fire Tower Committee
c/o Harry Jameson
P.O. Box 404
Phoenicia, N.Y. 12464
845-688-5553

Vanderwhacker Mountain
Friends of Vanderwhacker Fire Tower
c/o Noel Davis and Sue McMeekin
223 Perry Road
North Creek, N.Y. 12853
518-494-7000

Wakely Mountain
Friends of Wakely Mountain
c/o Bruce Lomnizer, Forest Ranger
NYS Department of Environmental Conservation
P.O. Box 5
Indian Lake, N.Y. 12842
518-648-5246

▶ *General Information on Adirondack and Catskill Fire Towers*

Adirondack Architectural Heritage (AARCH)
Attn. Steven Engelhart
1790 Main Street,
Civic Center, Suite 37
Keeseville, N.Y. 12944
518-834-9328

Adirondack Mountain Club (ADK)
Members Services Center
814 Goggins Rd.
Lake George, N.Y. 12845-4117
518-668-4447
www.adk.org

ADK Knickerbocker Chapter
www.adk-nyc.org/Firetowers.htm

Adirondack Museum
P.O. Box 99
Blue Mountain Lake, N.Y. 12812
518-352-7311

Catskill Center for Conservation and Development
Attn. Helen Budrock
Route 28
Arkville, N.Y. 12406
845-586-2611
www.catskilltowers.com

Forest Fire Lookout Association
Keith Argow, Chair
374 Maple Avenue E, Suite 310
Vienna, Va. 22180
703-255-2700
argow@nwoa.net
www.firelookout.org

Charles Vandrei
Historic Preservation Officer
NYS Department of Environmental Conservation
625 Broadway
Albany, N.Y. 12233-4255
518-402-9428
cevandre@gw.dec.state.ny.us

Martin Podskoch, author and historian
36 Waterhole Road
Colchester, CT 06415
860-267-2442
podskoch@adelphia.net

▶ *General Adirondack and Catskill Park Information*

Try the following for information and guidance on trail conditions, camping, safety, and Forest Preserve regulations.

Both Parks

NYS Department of Environmental Conservation (DEC)
www.dec.state.ny.us

New York State Public Campgrounds
Information: 518-457-2500
Reservations: 800-456-CAMP

Adirondack Park

DEC Region 5	*DEC Region 6*
Headquarters, Region 5	Headquarters, Region 6
Ray Brook, N.Y.	Watertown, N.Y.
518-897-1200	315-785-2245
Northville, N.Y.	Potsdam, N.Y. (St. Lawrence Co.)
518-863-4545	315-265-3090
Indian Lake, N.Y.	Herkimer, N.Y. (Herkimer Co.)
518-648-5616	315-866-6330
Warrensburg, N.Y.	Lowville, N.Y. (Lewis Co.)
518-668-5441	315-376-3521

Adirondack Visitor Interpretive Centers
NY 30, Box 3000
Paul Smiths, N.Y. 12970
518-327-3000

NY 28N, Box 101
Newcomb, N.Y. 12852
518-582-2000

Catskill Park

Ulster & Sullivan Counties
DEC Region 3 Headquarters
attn: George Profous, Senior Forester
21 South Putt Corners Rd.
New Paltz, N.Y. 12561
845-256-3000

Greene & Delaware Counties
DEC Region 4
attn: Paul Trotta, Regional Forester
Route 10
Stamford, N.Y. 12167
607-652-7365

Richard Parisio
DEC Environmental
Educator
Stony Kill Environmental
Center
79 Farmstead Lane
Wappingers Falls, NY 12590
845-831-8780 ext. 302
rfparisi@gw.dec.state.ny.us

Comparison of Route Difficulty

Ratings

▶ **Easy (1):**
Azure Mountain
Mount Arab
Bald Mountain (Rondaxe)
Belfry Mountain
Cathedral Rock
Red Hill

▶ **Moderate (2):**
Balsam Lake Mountain (via northern approach and southern loop approach)
Black Mountain (from the East)
Blue Mountain
Goodnow Mountain
Hadley Mountain
Hunter Mountain (via Colonel's Chair Trail)
Hunter Mountain (via Spruceton Trail)
Kane Mountain (both routes)
Overlook Mountain
Owls Head Mountain
Spruce Mountain
Mount Tremper (both routes)

▶ **Strenuous (3):**
Balsam Lake Mountain (via Mill Brook Ridge Trail)
Black Mountain (from Black Mountain Point)
Hunter Mountain (via Becker Hollow and Connector Trails)
Hurricane Mountain (all routes)
Lyon Mountain
Pillsbury Mountain
Poke-O-Moonshine Mountain
Snowy Mountain
St. Regis Mountain
Vanderwhacker Mountain
Wakely Mountain
Woodhull Mountain

▶ **Difficult (4):**
Mount Adams
Gore Mountain
Hunter Mountain (via Devil's Path and Hunter Mountain Spur Trail)

Index

Locations are listed by proper name with *Lake* or *Mount* following.

Acknowledgments

Let me first thank those who wrote—and endlessly revised—ADK's Forest Preserve Series of trail guides for the Adirondacks and Catskills, whose trail descriptions and maps provided the baseline for much of the work herein. They are *Laurence T. Cagle, Tony Goodwin, Art Haberl, Carl Heilman II, Linda Laing, Peter O'Shea, Bill Rudge, David Thomas-Train,* and *Bruce C. Wadsworth.* Thanks to Bruce Wadsworth also for permission to adapt some of the opening material from his book, *An Adirondack Sampler: Day Hikes for All Seasons.*

Thanks as well to those who helped compile descriptions for new and rerouted trails to the fire tower summits—*George and Helen Elias, Russ Guard, Carol Mantell,* and *Larry Rathman,* and to others who helped with updates to the text for particular summits—*Ted Comstock, Peter Curtiss, Steven Engelhart, Roy Fordham,* and *Herbert Hudnut Jr.*

The fine essay on the history of fire towers in the Adirondack and Catskill regions was written by professional historic preservationist *Wes Haynes,* and used with the kind permission of *Adirondack Architectural Heritage (AARCH)*, the region's not-for-profit historic preservation organization. AARCH commissioned Wes's work for nominations of ten of these towers to the National Register of Historic Places. AARCH has also formed a financial partnership with "Friends" restoration groups for Mt. Arab and Poke-O-Moonshine.

Not-for-profit status was made available to restorations at Blue and Hadley Mountains as projects of the *Cornell Cooperative Extension of Hamilton and Saratoga Counties,* respectively. Restorations in the Catskills would not have had the focus nor been accomplished with nearly the speed without the organizational help and financial sponsorship of the *Catskill Center for Conservation and Development.*

Special thanks to other citizens whose paths I've crossed in tower restoration work in the last seven years. Their energy and enthusiasm has been an inspiration to each other and to me. They include *Jim Briggs, Helen Budrock, Dave Cutter, Dave Deitze, Gerald and Sherry Dobbs, Raymond Dumas, Darwin Gensel, Peter Gucker, Barbara Haspiel, Inverna Lockpez, Fred and Teddy Margulies, Ray Masters, Don Mauer, Richard Mooers, Gerald Morrow, Dick and Peggy Purdue, Kermit Remele, Andrew Saunders, Leo Smith, Jack Swan, David Thomas-Train,* and scores of others.

The support of staff members of the *Adirondack Mountain Club* has greatly enhanced fire tower rehab work, trail improvement to the towers, and educational programs geared to the refurbished towers. My thanks to *Jo Benton, Karen Brooks* (and for her splendid page maps), *Bill Brosseau, Anne Green, Andrea Masters* (who inspired this book), *Carol Shaw, Vicki Sweet, Tim Tierney,* and especially *Neil Woodworth,* whose impetus at Blue Mountain in 1993 inspired restorations at Hadley Mountain, Mount Arab, and Poke-O-Moonshine.

Everyone interested in fire towers owes gratitude to those *NYS Department of Environmental Conservation forest rangers, foresters, and regional managers* who squeezed in time for meetings with citizen restoration committees, and in several instances, rolled up their sleeves and worked directly on restoration projects. They include *Tom Monroe, Terry Healy, Stewart Brown, Rick Dearstyne, Gary Friedrich, Greg George, Fred Gerty, Jeff Gregg, Steve Guenther, Charles Platt, George Profous, David Smith, Paul Trotta, Charles Vandrei* (Historic Preservation Officer), and *Pat Whalen.*

And finally, I would be remiss if I did not cite those special friends who have helped with encouragement and technical advice: *Tillie Helms, Nancy Hudnut,* and *Dorothy Verhagen.*

Jack Freeman
Glens Falls, New York
May 2001

Biographies

John P. (Jack) Freeman has worked for eight years in conservation affairs for the Adirondack Mountain Club, following a career in photographic chemistry with the Eastman Kodak Company. An avid hiker, he is an Adirondack Winter 46er who has also ascended the high points of

all fifty states. A leading voice in efforts to restore fire towers in the New York State Forest Preserve, Jack has offered slide show presentations on fire towers before numerous audiences, and in doing so, helped spark new interest in these compelling structures.

Jack claims that his three chemistry degrees have done virtually nothing to qualify him to assemble this guidebook. He credits his friends for insisting he try and for helping.

Wesley H. Haynes holds an undergraduate degree in historical geography from Clark University and an M.S. in Historic Preservation from the School of Architecture and Planning at Columbia University. Wes has studied the indigenous and imported architecture of the Adirondacks for 20 years. In the course of his work, he has researched and authored essays resulting in the designation of Sagamore Lodge and Camp Santanoni as National Historic Landmarks, the highest level of federal recognition of a historic resource. His efforts have also led to the listing of New York State Forest Preserve fire towers on the State Register of Historic Places. National Register listing is also expected as of this writing (2001).

Wes has served as a preservation planner in the restoration of the New York State Capitol in Albany and is currently a program officer with the New Jersey Historic Trust and an adjunct professor of Building Conservation at Rensselaer Polytechnic Institute.

Backdoor to Backcountry

ADKers choose from friendly outings, for those just getting started with local chapters, to Adirondack backpacks and international treks. Learn gradually through chapter outings or attend one of our schools, workshops, or other programs. A sampling includes:

- Alpine Flora
- Ice Climbing
- Rock Climbing
- Basic Canoeing/Kayaking
- Bicycle Touring
- Cross-country Skiing and snowshoeing
- Mountain Photography
- Winter Mountaineering
- Birds of the Adirondacks
- Geology of the High Peaks
  ... and so much more!

For more information:
ADK Member Services Center
(Exit 21 off the Northway, I-87)
814 Goggins Rd., Lake George, NY 12845-4117

ADK Heart Lake Program Center
P.O. Box 867, Lake Placid, NY 12946-0867

Information: 518-668-4447
Membership: 800-395-8080
Publications and merchandise: 800-395-8080
Education: 518-523-3441
Facilities' reservation: 518-523-3441
E-mail: adkinfo@adk.org
Web site: www.adk.org

Join Us

We are a nonprofit membership organization that brings together people with interests in recreation, conservation, and environmental education in the New York State Forest Preserve.

Membership Benefits

- **Discovery:**
  ADK can broaden your horizons by introducing you to new places, recreational activities, and interests.

- **Enjoyment:**
  Being outdoors more and loving it more.

- **People:**
  Meeting others and sharing the fun.

- *Adirondac* Magazine.

- **Member Discounts:**
  20% off on guidebooks, maps, and other ADK publications; discount on lodge stays; discount on educational programs.

- **Satisfaction:**
  Knowing you're doing your part and that future generations will enjoy the wilderness as you do.

- **Chapter Participation:**
  Brings you the fun of outings and other social activities and the reward of working on trails, conservation, and education projects at the local level. You can also join as a member at large. Either way, all Club activities and benefits are available.